THE *Rhinestone* SISTERHOOD

ALSO BY DAVID VALDES GREENWOOD

Homo Domesticus

A Little Fruitcake

THE

Rhinestone

SISTERHOOD

★

A Journey Through Small-Town
America, One Tiara at a Time

DAVID VALDES GREENWOOD

CROWN PUBLISHERS

New York

Published in the United States by Crown Publishers, an imprint
of the Crown Publishing Group, a division of Random House,
Inc., New York.

www.crownpublishing.com

Crown is a trademark and the Crown colophon is a registered
trademark of Random House, Inc.

Library of Congress Cataloging-in-Publication Data
Valdes Greenwood, David.
Rhinestone sisterhood / David Valdes Greenwood.—1st ed.
1. Beauty contests—United States.   2. Beauty contestants—
United States.   3. Girls—United States—Social life and
customs.   I. Title.
HQ1220.U5V35 2010
306.4'8—dc22   2009044994

ISBN 978-0-307-46527-6

Printed in the United States of America

10 9 8 7 6 5 4 3 2 1

First Edition

To
four queens,
a diva,
and
my little princess

GATHERING QUEENS

Tradition cannot be purchased
Like a set of dishes,
Or a kitchen appliance.
Heritage must be preserved;
Often it must be rescued.
Or it must be created.

> —*Carolyn Cunha Granelli,*
> *1921 Half Moon Bay Chamarita*
> *Festival Queen*

Crown Chasers Need Not Apply

Chelsea Richard is crying. A tiny thing, a sparrow wrapped in pink silk, she is visibly shaking, not with sorrow or anger, but frustration pure and deep. She bolts out of the pageant interview room, her eyes filling rapidly as if each step she takes pumps tears. Seconds ago, three judges finished grilling her about why they should place a crystal-studded crown on her head tonight, why they should trust her—as opposed to one of the other four girls lined up—to represent their festival for the coming year. The actual pageant isn't for hours yet, but her make-or-break moment is already over. That interview, which alone counts for half of her score, is the only chance she has to make a distinct personal impression on the judges without her competition in their line of sight. She spent two years dreaming of how to handle that moment, and now she's sure she's blown it.

At just over five feet tall, and weighing less than a hundred pounds, Chelsea's slim frame displays anxiety in the way a reed trembles in the face of a strong wind. None of the pageant volunteers approach her to offer comfort, knowing what would happen if they did: The eternal gossip—that every pageant is rigged—would have new kindling. Like the other girls, Chelsea is here for the interview alone, no parents or friends yet in tow to soothe her. She tries to get control of her feelings, to stop the tears simply by blinking them away, and fails. "I messed it up. Why can't I just say what I'm feeling?" Her voice is nearly impossible to hear. "I *need* this."

What she needs, what she desires enough to risk such loss and pain, is to be Frog Queen.

It's a prospect appealing enough to convince five girls to don two- and three-piece business suits on this cloying ninety-four-degree August day. They have gathered for closed-door interviews here at the Rayne Civic Center and RV Park, the last place you'd think to look for a little sparkle. The building oozes municipal practicality, the very essence of anti-glamour: a pale mustard auditorium that doesn't so much rise as squat wide on its flat tract, surrounded by a sun-baked terrain punctuated with hook-ups for Winnebagos and Airstreams. Just inside the front entry, a set of double doors hides the room where three panelists sit behind a long folding table interviewing the slim slate of contestants who hope to become the public face of the Rayne Frog Festival, the four summer days that are the centerpiece of the Louisiana town's civic identity.

As each girl enters the judging room, the others drift around the empty arena fighting butterflies and killing the slow minutes by themselves. Pageant volunteers collect the girls' paperwork but otherwise leave them to their own devices, so as to avoid starting favoritism rumors on the Voy boards, an online forum with vicious rooms dedicated to pageants statewide. Being at loose ends seems to unsettle Christana, the youngest competitor. A model of graciousness, "Yes, ma'am" and "No, sir" passing her lips as unconsciously as breath, she nonetheless can't rest; she doesn't sit down at any of the frog-decorated tables set up for tonight's audience, preferring to remain standing, shifting nervously from foot to foot.

Christana's thick dark hair is styled in a heavy wave that makes her look much older than seventeen, but when she speaks, her voice is still that of a tender girl. She's not from Rayne—in fact, she's not from a town at all. Though she spent many hours in Rayne as a child, her family lives in an unincorporated hamlet too small for a name of its own. About to begin her senior year, she has been home-schooled her whole life, which she likes because she's smart enough to blow through her full day's course load in three hours, leaving the rest of the day free to ride horses in dreams of being an Olympic rider. So why take time away from the barn to follow the pageant path? The first answer out of her mouth is telling: "Well, I want to meet new people"—a fair concern for a girl with no classmates. So far, her greatest opportunity for socialization has been as a dancer for the International Rice Festival, which leads to the tale of how when her troupe came to perform at Rayne's festival, she found a frog inside her hat and shrieked with fear. Maybe she shouldn't tell that story to judges in a town built on the frog-leg export industry.

Sondra, as dark as Christana is fair, wears her nervous energy differently. If a human could throw sparks, the twenty-one-year-old would, emitting a combination of internal curiosity and electric enthusiasm. She is the only contestant of color, hasn't competed before, and admits she doesn't yet know how to finesse a pageant, but she flashes a kilowatt smile nonetheless. Sondra has never been to the Frog Festival or Rayne in her twenty-one years, but she keeps hearing, "There's no festival like Frog." So here she is, in her best suit and brightest smile, waiting for her chance to wow the judges. She has come armed with knowledge of the town's economic underpinnings, how the festival funds the Chamber of Commerce, and how revenue from the RV park keeps the fire department and police force running. A business major with plans for an MBA, she says she first wants to use her degree to combat poverty and then to be president of the United States. Between now and the White House, she says, "I just hope to be happy in anything I choose. What good is making millions if I'm not happy?" (She doesn't doubt she could make millions—she just wonders whether she wants to.)

Confidence is also on full display as a fourth contestant, Hope, nears her turn for interview. Standing five-foot-eight in her heels, with Mae West curves filling out a sleek pearl satin ensemble, Hope looks like a future first lady, and her hair has been coiffed in perfect Jackie O fashion. Still a teenager, she has nonetheless already collected a few titles, which she lists in a sentence at once perfectly logical and yet bordering on sort of Dada poetry: "I was Mayhaw, that's a berry, and Church Buggy, and hopefully now Frog." She intends to impress the judges by describing the community service she does when not in cosmetology classes. "I work with younger people through modeling and giving haircuts to the less fortunate." Before she can explain how one works with youth through modeling, she is called to the judges' chamber and slips inside, perfectly poised for success.

Less polished but sunnier is Jennifer, a nineteen-year-old who, like the others, wears a suit, but otherwise looks like she might have run in from a game of soccer. She hasn't filled out all her paperwork and apologizes with a hapless cheer. Her wheat-colored hair is pulled messily into a ponytail, a few stray strands unsure where they belong, yet it doesn't matter at all. She conveys a beauty that seems to have nothing to do with her looks. At nearly six feet tall, she bounces when she walks and seems to be laughing even when she isn't.

Just two weeks ago, Jennifer completed her year as Miss Rayne, a civic crown that involves working in the mayor's office. It is a traditional requirement for Miss Rayne that she compete for the title of Frog Queen in the first pageant after her civic term ends, and many local people believe she should get special consideration because of her proven service. But Jennifer says that she would have competed even if it hadn't been required. Projecting contagious buoyancy, her speech is punctuated with audible exclamation marks. "Ever since I was little, I loved to play with frogs! Kids would say, 'You'll get warts!' But that never bothered me. One year when the Frog Queen wasn't available, I was asked if I'd kiss a frog for a camera crew and I just puckered right up!" Neutral or not, every pageant volunteer who passes by says hello to Jennifer by name.

Jennifer's popularity is unknown to the contestants save Chelsea, the only other local girl. But Chelsea also knows that having been Miss Rayne is no guarantee of victory at Frog: Twelve months ago, Chelsea was the most recent Miss Rayne—in fact, she herself crowned Jennifer—but that didn't do her a lick of good at last year's Frog pageant, where she not only lost, but lost to an outsider, after an interview just like this.

Her town's titles mean something to Chelsea: She was Frog Derby Queen before she was Miss Rayne. But this is the big one, the title she wants most. This weekend, she could be competing for a festival title in another town—the Duck and Gumbo pageants are today, too—but she doesn't want just any old crown: It *has* to be Frog. So she does what she can: She dries her eyes, straightens her suit, and tries to put on a brave face, joking about the kind of inspirational mantras she adopted the first time she lost. " 'Everything happens for a reason' was what I told myself *last* year. I guess I'll just have to Google a new line tonight." But in her heart, she isn't ready to surrender the crown, not just yet. She bites her lip. "Maybe I can still pull it off onstage . . ." Perhaps she even believes it.

If she really has blown her chance with the judges, it won't be easy to recover: The offstage interview yields more points than any other single element of competition. The two primary components of tonight's pageant, the public intro-duction each girl makes for herself and then her grace as she models (the official term for walking the stage in her evening gown), are together worth fewer points than the afternoon's questioning. That's because a queen's primary role is not to be pretty but to be persuasive: The Frog Queen is not a beauty pageant winner but a civic representative. As a festival queen, she will spend the next year selling this town and its festival to strangers all over the state, and if she fails, no one will care how lovely she looked along the way. A knowledgeable girl who blows the judges away in private is likely to be unstoppable, no matter how she does onstage. This is why festival queens, unlike traditional beauty queens, come in all shapes and sizes. Only when there is no clear star in the afternoon can the evening make a truly significant difference. By the time the final element of the pageant, an onstage interview, takes place, a mere twenty points hang in the balance. Those points will never take a fourth-place girl into the lead, but they can decide a close race.

For now, one thing is clear: Jennifer has enjoyed her interview more than Chelsea. The last contestant put through her paces, Jennifer exhibits not a trace of worry on her open face when she finishes. She radiates cheer as she returns, though she says it's not about how well she did, she's just happy to be able to get out of the suit. And then she's out the front door, striding away on long legs born to skip.

Evening falls, but the air in Rayne has barely cooled, despite a stunningly loud afternoon thunderstorm that knocked on the ceilings of the town's low roofs and then moved across the prairie. By five P.M., the sun is heavier in the sky but still bright, so that it takes a moment for one's eyes to adjust upon entering the Civic Center. Inside, a luminescent sea of colored silk swells in living waves. A hundred and five Visiting Queens from across the state have gathered for the competition, the rhinestones of their tall tiaras reflecting upward into the glass backboards of retracted basketball hoops, while their jewel-beaded trains sweep across the free-throw lines beneath their feet.

Satin banners, as their sashes are known, announce Teen, Miss, and Ms. royalty representing every conceivable festival domain: There are queens of things you grow (from Oranges to Watermelon) and things you farm (Rabbit, Cattle, and Swine), princesses of industry (Cotton and Timber) and transportation (Railroad, Steamboat, and Buggy), dual-purpose royalty with ampersands on their banners (Shrimp & Petroleum, Oil & Gas, Fur & Wildlife), as well as queens of beloved Cajun foods (Etouffée and Jambalaya). There are even enough recipe ingredients (Spice, Crawfish, Catfish, Smoked Meat, and Rice) that we're just a celery queen shy of gumbo. (Actually, there *is* a Gumbo Queen, but she couldn't make it.)

This is the Rhinestone Sisterhood, the rolling sorority of new friends a girl joins when she wins a festival queen title. The winners' primary duties extend beyond their sponsoring towns: They attend one another's festivals and pageants, week after week, for an entire year. Spending so many long days with their new sister queens, they form bonds that often last a lifetime. Some end up rooming together in college, walking down the aisle in bridesmaid dresses at one another's weddings, going into business together, or playing Auntie to one another's children.

These queens are not an afterthought, but part of the pageant's pomp and circumstance. Later tonight every single one of them will cross the stage as they are introduced by name and title in a roll call so long it'll be broken into three waves. In an event with no live band, they are de facto rock stars, adding the imprint of celebrity to an otherwise homespun affair. The effect of their presence is already clear: An awestruck gaggle of little girls in Sunday dresses point at this queen's dress or that one's crown, their young eyes aglow with the possibility of a future so shiny. The Fur Queen sees them pointing and smiles, then crouches (as much as her gown allows such a thing) to say hello, one hand extended in greeting, the other making sure her crown doesn't fall clear off her head.

As these queens move toward seats reserved just for their shimmering ranks, the rest of the hall fills with the families and friends of contestants, a few wearing appropriately amphibious green and some carrying their own frogabilia, but most dressed in street clothes or relaxed church attire. Some in the audience have brought their own spreads, picnics that will fan out across their tables as they settle in for a lengthy twofer pageant that will crown not only the Miss but her Teen counterpart as well. For those who didn't pack a meal, snacks are on sale, including tub after tub stocked with cold cans of Budweiser, which outsell even the brownies. Some attendees have even brought their own frozen cocktails from the drive-through daiquiri bar in town (where the straw is handed to customers separately, so as to discourage drinking and driving).

Amid the ebb and flow of the crowds, Cheryl McCarty directs traffic. At forty-five, Ms. Cheryl, as the girls call her, is a one-woman epicenter of volunteerism and civic pride. As the town's cultural director (a position she made up and then talked the mayor into creating), Ms. Cheryl's likely to be in the thick of any event in town that draws a crowd: She runs the pageant, the festival, a fishing derby, summer camp, a cancer fund-raiser, and Rayne's Halloween celebration. But she sure doesn't read like a PTA mom or a stereotypical small-town do-gooder. She doesn't wear knit sweaters with seasonal patterns or chirp cheery slogans. With her mane of red hair and full curves, she's decidedly more va-va-voom than Church Lady. In leopard prints, leather jacket, and sky-high heels, she makes the ladies of Wisteria Lane look a little dull. She's a Red Hot Mama with the gift of gab *and* a will of steel, the living model of what many festival queens hope to become: a woman of power who still enjoys playing dress-up.

She'd seem larger than life in most towns, but in Rayne everyone you meet knows Ms. Cheryl. That familiarity means, of course, that she can't judge the pageant or have any say in who gets picked. Nonetheless, she knows what she wants. "A real Frog Queen does it for the right reasons: She believes in community first and she also believes in tourism. And she understands the value to the community of the economic benefits from that tourism." That's hardly the stereotypical description of pageant queens propagated by the media: dumb girls with big hair and nothing more to offer than the ability to fill out a pretty dress while standing upright in heels. "The girls who do well are the ones who are passionate about what they represent, who feel it in their heart and give it everything they've got."

But Ms. Cheryl freely admits that not every girl on the festival circuit is so pure in her ambitions. "We have what we call 'Crown Chasers,' who will do anything to win. They collect titles wherever they can but don't really care about the festivals. That's why our contract allows you to be queen of *only* this festival until your year is done. We don't want any 'weekend specials,' girls who hold three titles at once so the town never sees them again until the next pageant."

Last year's winner, Amanda, wasn't a Rayne girl, and in fact lives an hour away, but she was just the kind of queen Ms. Cheryl likes, having logged forty-four events in fifty-two weeks. It wasn't her first time as a queen; Amanda had also been Miss Contraband Days, reigning over a festival devoted to a historic Gulf Coast pirate. But she says Frog has been special. "I tell the girls everywhere: You've *got* to go to Rayne. They let me be involved in *everything*." Two hours away from handing over her title, the soon-to-be ex-queen is both proud and wistful. "You just can't top this."

As Amanda hurries by, her crown in place, Ms. Cheryl notices something missing. "You gonna come in with your train and mantle? You have four minutes." Amanda doesn't argue— no one argues with Ms. Cheryl. The train in question, a floor-length cape that stretches several yards behind the queen as she walks, is part of the queen's official regalia, which also includes a $1,500 crown and a heavy jewel-encrusted mantle that gets strapped on under her arms and then rises behind her head like a stiff, glittering web. Amanda may need the entire four minutes just to get the outfit on.

In the greenroom, which really is just a smaller auditorium off the main room, the girls make nice—even as they try to size up their chances. Sondra makes a terrific impression, chatting easily and with warmth, winning over her new peers. Hope has the opposite effect: She spends so much time talking about her modeling career that some of her fellow contestants think she wants to be a beauty queen, not the representative of a local festival. Chelsea is not crazy about Hope's attitude and begins to think that if she herself can't win, maybe the best thing would be for the title to go to Jennifer. They're not friends, but at least the crown would be worn by a girl sure to do right by Rayne.

Beyond the cocoon of the greenroom, cameras are everywhere. The town's two warring newspapers have sent photographers lugging heavy, bricklike shutters, while little children wield instant cameras that look like toys, and at least one royal boyfriend is stationed on the front lines with a home camcorder. Most noticeable are the mothers, visibly eager to document every moment of the night in which their daughters enter the stream of local tradition. Outgoing Teen Frog Queen Sarah calls these women the Mamarazzi, and Ms. Cheryl has to keep them in line, announcing appropriate times for the swarm of misty-eyed shutterbugs to descend—but only after the official journalists have their turn. Like their girls, the Mamarazzi are all part of one pack for now, but at the end of the night, one of them will join another club: Queen Moms, who share in the travels and royal duties nearly as intensely as their daughters, if from behind the scenes.

The lights dim a bit to signal that the time has come to get started. The five Miss girls and eight Teens enter and sit at floor level in plastic chairs at one side of the temporary runway set up beneath the basketball hoop. Just ahead of the contestants, the three judges sit facing the twelve-foot catwalk, their backs to the seated girls, which means that a competitor will never be privy to a judge's expressions of approval or dismay except when she herself is facing them. What the girls *can* see is the veritable mountain range of Visiting Queens, their crowns forming gem-crusted peaks on the opposite side of the runway.

Even among those ranks, there is a hierarchy: Every girl here wants to be Brandi Stout. A vivacious girl with a natural ease around others, she's a role model not just because she is Tamale Queen, as her banner reads, but because she also possesses the heavy and much-coveted crown that reveals her to be the Queen of Queens. This is the ultimate title, earned in a queen-off of epic proportions held in the state capital every year. Come February, the girl who wins Frog tonight will compete to replace Brandi or at least earn a spot in the Top 15, an honor rewarded with a ruby-red pin to display on her queen's banner ever after. At a glance, the Top 15 pin announces its wearer as the cream of the crop, the Rhinestone Varsity first string.

Of the girls competing at the Civic Center today, only Hope has a ruby pin. At the pageant that crowned Brandi just months ago, Hope placed sixth, an impressive achievement that might well make her the favorite here at Frog, except that an out-of-town girl is only likely to win in Rayne when her personality captures attention as much as her skill on heels. Right now it's Jennifer who's getting the good buzz. She's the only girl whose fans have brought homemade signs—WE LOVE JENNIFER!—and every move she makes earns applause. Two women in the front nod approvingly as she enters, one whispering loud enough to be heard, "She's got this in the bag!"

That opinion is not shared universally. Next to me, Ms. Cheryl's boyfriend, Miles Boudreaux, thinks Jennifer will go down as a near-miss. A burly twenty-nine-year-old who played high-school football (he was the pulling guard for future Houston Texan Dominick Davis), Miles is most impressed by Hope, who does indeed look incredibly polished in a snug black gown, which works a certain magic by saving all its jewels for the bustline.

But once the pageant is under way, it seems almost anybody's game. As a skinny DJ in a skull-shrinking ball cap, white T-shirt, and jeans spins soft rock and country pop on a turntable, the contestants take their first walk onstage and introduce themselves, each offering herself up to the crowd in her final line as "your contestant." Wearing a black strapless gown ending in a cascade of lace ruffles, Sondra is a vision of composure, and she sets the rhetorical bar high as well, announcing that "the world was built to develop character."

Cheers follow her, and the crowd seems smitten with this outsider now. In the time it takes her to complete her walk, the sentiment in the room has shifted from "*Who* is she?" to "Who *is* she?"

It's a tough act to follow, and Christana seems crippled by it, unable to get out her first line, "From Rayne's humble beginning . . ." A gargling sound stops her. "Uh, I am so sorry about that. From Rayne's humble beginning . . ." And she goes on this time, but her voice is shaking, and when she exits, her posture gives way for a moment. The contrast with Hope couldn't be clearer; Hope moves into place so efficiently it seems as if she is carried aboard an unseen dolly. When she says her hobby is "froggin'," she sounds so sincere that I almost believe it. A din of whoops and cheers follows her to her seat.

It is clear Chelsea wants to keep her speech frogalicious: It is full of punny phrases like "have an un-frog-ettable time," and she gets laughs from the audience when she notes that "our frogs are not only tasty snacks but great astronauts." It's not just the joke itself that sells, it's the use of "our frogs," a phrase she gets into her monologue four or five times. This reminds the crowd of two things: Not just any frogs will do, and the superior frogs of Rayne are theirs and *hers,* unlike some of the girls they will meet tonight. From a marketing angle, this is smart branding (which, after all, is what her job will entail should she win). Even so, the local-girl angle may favor Jennifer, clad in frog-green silk, who opens with, "Got Frog? Rayne does!" and earns the loudest cries of adoration, perhaps less for her solid speech than for simply being up where all her fans can see.

As Sarah McLachlan's "Angel" lulls the crowd, now an hour into the evening, the contestants walk the line before the judges. The girls seem to have strategies in mind, Sondra making sure to flash her sweetest smile at the crowd before making eye contact with the judges, while Hope earns the royalty vote by taking time to give a regal nod of appreciation in the direction of the Visiting Queens. Chelsea fairly glides down the runway, an ethereal blue ribbon in motion, while Jennifer simply walks forward and, grinning, leans into the love of the audience. Christana has regained her spine, but her movements are constricted, and when she comes down the stairs, she exhales her held breath like a woman newly released from a hostage situation. And then the girls wait.

Lee Ann Womack and the Carpenters croon inspiring platitudes, a sound track meant to soothe, which only makes the moments feel even longer while the judges confer. These three women are the only people who know whether this is a close competition or not. To avoid conflicts of interest, none of them are current Rayne residents. The first judge runs two other festival pageants, Hot Sauce and Shrimp, so she comes with a focus on festival needs. The second judge coordinates the team dancers for the New Orleans Zephyrs and Hornets, and wants a girl who can handle the spotlight. The third judge is the only one who has ever lived here, though she has since moved twice and now lives more than two hundred miles away, in Shreveport. Having herself amassed a list of festival titles a half-mile long (among them not only Frog but Swine and Cattle), Brooke Henry is more than qualified to judge, but if either Jennifer or Chelsea wins, Brooke knows she'll get accused of local bias even so.

After the judges have conferred, the mayor—known to everyone as Jimbo—takes the stage, which is when the drama typically ends for most of the competitors. This is when the four finalists are supposed to be announced, and normally only those girls are invited to join him for an onstage interview that will determine the decisive final ten points of the evening. But with so few girls running tonight, the judges have decided it would be cruel to leave one girl alone and invite the rest up, so all five prepare for their last shot, even though one of these stories won't do its teller a bit of good. As the girls prepare to deliver their "lighthearted topics," as the final question is known, Mayor Jimbo and Ms. Cheryl engage in a teasing banter in which the mayor delivers self-deprecating remarks and Ms. Cheryl plays the part of the diva amused by her funny little man—think Sonny and Cher on steroids.

When it's her turn to speak, Sondra has no problem keeping up, telling the mayor that he's met his match, as she launches into a story about hobbling around the first day of college on one heel, followed closely by a story in which she falls into the water while fishing. The Visiting Queens see her with new eyes, visibly envious of her ability to tell a story, and for the first time all night, they applaud for her as loudly as the audience does. Seeing how well Sondra's mishap stories landed, Christana launches into a tale of how her entire family had a skiing accident, but the telling is slow and overlong, and you can feel hundreds of people willing her to finish. Catfish especially, perhaps forgetting she is in the front row and thus visible, listens to the unending story with her lips apart in a horrified "O," her brows furrowed, the look of someone watching a car crash in slow motion. But nothing compares to the misfire of Hope, who chooses to endear herself to the audience by telling them that it wasn't until this year that she understood how hard it is to be a model, that ten-hour days in heels is a terrible burden. Miles shakes his head at this gem from his initial pick and whispers, "Well, then again . . ."

The last two girls know Mayor Jimbo, who has run the town since they were children. That changes the dynamic to an extent, with Chelsea newly confident enough to straighten the mayor's shoulders as she tells him how he can make sure that people like him in ninety seconds. When she warns him never to lose his posture, he fires back, "If I lose my posture, something's definitely gonna hang out," a bawdy line that elicits a roar of laughter from the crowd. Unwilling to be upstaged, she puts the mayor in his place and forges on as if this is *her* show, which, of course, it has to be. She leaves the runway to the most applause she has received all night. Interview, it turns out, is her forte after all. If she sounded like this behind closed doors as well, perhaps all those tears were for nothing.

It is hard to say whether it is a good or bad gambit for Jennifer to begin by noting that, in kindergarten, she broke the mayor's daughter's arm. It's a personal touch, but maybe too personal, one of those winking we-go-back-a-long-way flourishes that can set off those infernal rumors: If she wins tonight, the Voy boards will use this story as evidence that the whole thing was rigged. Her main story is about a boy who wanted Popeye's fried chicken from Santa, but the tale, amusing as it may be, goes on nearly as long as Christana's ski accident monologue. This late in the night—the pageant is now past the two-hour mark—it seems like a lot to ask of the audience, but they scream themselves hoarse and wave their GO #5! signs, anyway.

Restless children and grown-ups alike are now wandering about the Civic Center, and table whispers have become an incessant buzz of chatter. Lengthy tape-recorded speeches accompany the final walks of the outgoing queens, who pass out roses to all their loved ones, a ritual sweet for those involved, if something of an endurance test for everyone else. As Amanda's last piece of advice—"Put some cushion on this crown, 'cause it hurts"—rings out from the loudspeakers, Ms. Cheryl is finally handed the results.

The girls stand, their whole beings inclining toward the stage. The first announcement is of Miss Congeniality, chosen by the competitors instead of the judges. For that honor, the contestants have picked Christana, which is good, as the judges have not selected her for anything else. When the 3rd Maid is announced, the bottom of the court, it turns out to be Sondra, and it's clear that the audience would have ranked her higher. But she glows nonetheless, a feat that Hope cannot quite pull off when called forward as 2nd Maid. Her eyes are darker than they were just moments ago; the dream she came here for, the literal mantle she can see from where she stands, will belong to someone else. She is now just one-third of a trio wearing the sweet-sad smiles of those who already know they will leave this auditorium tonight with flowers instead of a crown.

Only two girls remain.

They are called onto the stage, where they stand thrilled and shaking. These are the Rayne girls, the ones everybody knows. Chelsea and Jennifer entwine their slim fingers, as Amanda takes up station behind them, her newly relinquished crown poised midair. Hundreds of us—parents, boyfriends, neighbors, strangers—are caught up in the question of this moment, the spell that every pageant comes down to in its final seconds, the held breath before the answer to the great mystery is exhaled.

Who will be Frog Queen?

2

Meet the Frog Queen

That girl in the shop at the mall, the one helping you find your size—she's one. The young fast-food worker, her hair up in a webbed net as she keeps the chicken fingers flying—she's one. The freshman who smuggles a thermos the size of her arm into the library to cram for her bio midterm—she's one. The cowgirl mucking stalls, the barista at Starbucks, the band captain, the valedictorian, the babysitter, and the girl who bags your groceries at Piggly Wiggly—all of them, festival queens. In some parts of the country, they're everywhere you go, but without their regalia, you'd never know you're in the presence of royalty.

If you want to find America's small-town festival queens, the best place to look is Louisiana. And there's perhaps nowhere better than Rayne to get started. Pageant affection runs deep here. According to Ms. Cheryl, "We have frog titles from the cradle to the grave!" Children under six compete for Miss and Mr. Tadpole, while seven- to nine-year-old girls aim for Deb Frog Princess and ten- to twelve-year-olds aim for the satiny green mantle of the Junior Frog Queen. Thirteen- to sixteen-year-olds, still coming into their own and dwarfed by their cotillion-worthy dresses, vie for Teen Frog Queen. Ms. Frog Queen attracts women in their thirties or forties, and even senior citizens get in the act as Golden Frogs, with both a king and a queen. Did I mention the Frog Derby Queen—a girl in a racing outfit? Or the Frog Jockey Queen, who represents Rayne at the Rice Festival in neighboring Crowley? And that's just *frog* royalty. (In addition to Miss Rayne, the title held by Chelsea and Jennifer both, there's also a children's festival queen.)

Even here, though, not all royals are created equal. One queen rules over the rest: the winner of the Miss division, composed of high-school girls and college students age seventeen to twenty-three. She gets both the longest list of duties and the nicest crown, as well as the most opportunities to officially represent Frog City all over the state. Tadpoles, Debs, Juniors, and Teens grow up wanting to someday be her—and, eventually, at least one or two of them will be. For a year, she's the emerald shining star of her town and everybody knows it. You can tell this in how they refer to her; though officially she's Miss Rayne Frog Festival Queen, nobody calls her that. The word *festival* is dropped universally in conversation about winners, but while every other titleholder continues to be referred to by a qualifying adjective—Deb Frog or Ms. Frog—the word *Miss* disappears once she is crowned, no further explanation needed. When someone says "Frog Queen" in Rayne, it doesn't matter how many tiaras fill the room: You *know* who they mean.

It's no small thing to be Frog Queen in this town. Take the

Rayne exit off I-10 and you will see frogabilia everywhere. Restaurants are amphibiously themed, from Chef Roy's Frog City Café to Frog City Plaza, the fancy name for the convenience store that locals just call "the truck stop." You can order frog legs from the drive-through window at Gabe's or buy frog-print attire at the dollar store. Head down the main drag and you'll be greeted by a thirteen-foot-tall aluminum sculpture of Monsieur Jacques, the town's frog mascot, as well as FROG X-ING signs, a frog fountain, and wall after wall frescoed with the green beasts dressed as lawyers or schoolchildren or shopkeepers. To this day, frogs are the main tourist attraction in Rayne, luring forty thousand outsiders a year to its annual Frog Festival, where the Frog Queen reigns supreme.

As evidenced by the turnout for her pageant, the Frog Queen isn't remotely alone. In Louisiana, she has sister queens named for everything from Smoked Meat to Petroleum. She'll likely never meet Miss Fire Ant in Georgia or the Watermelon Thump Queen of Texas, let alone the many Dairy Maids and Princesses who fill the American heartland, but they share many of the same attributes nonetheless. For one thing, these girls *are* girls, not clever drag queens with titles premised on puns or innuendo. But they're not traditional beauty queens, either, parading in bathing suits or tap-dancing to "Stars and Stripes Forever." Acting as small-town ambassadors, they're just as comfortable mucking about in fields and barns in rubber boots as they are onstage in evening gowns and enormous, elaborate crowns.

And it's not just Louisiana, or the South in general, that

remains full of young royals: Ohio has more than sixty, for instance, and Washington State has dozens. From the Carolinas to California, agricultural and industrial festivals crown queens (and, in some regions, attendants) who are then dispatched as ambassadors to events at the far reaches of their states. Collectively, they are all known as royalty, while each festival's specific set of emissaries—trios and quartets mostly, but even sextets and octets—is called its court. From Florida to Wisconsin, Oregon to Maine, local girls pack up newly won crowns and rafts of knowledge about their festivals and hit the country roads every weekend of the warmer months.

These queens are the embodiment of local spirit, representing some town or county's greatest resource. The girls don't just get a crown and adoration and a little cash, they have to work for all of it. To win their titles, they must first prove their knowledge of decidedly unglamorous subjects from meat-packing to animal-skinning, and convince the judges that they can spend a year sharing their knowledge. For some of the smallest towns, these queens might well be the lone ambassadors, the only kind of advertising that an out-of-the-way community can afford as a way of attracting visitors. At the same time, they are the living face of local tradition, sometimes wearing crowns their own friends and family wore before them. These aren't damsels in distress, they're sisters doing it (not just) for themselves. It may be hard to see all this past the glint of sunlight on sequins as a royal float rolls down the Main Street of a tiny town, but it's true.

While festivals themselves are traditionally linked to one

particular town, their queens may not always be. Some festivals do limit applicants to residents of one town or region, but many pageants will accept a girl from anywhere in the state so long as she can prove to the very serious judges that she knows the history of the host town and its festival, and can sell residents of other towns on the virtues of both; she must also persuasively commit herself to showing up all year long for events in the town that crowns her. That's how it is in Rayne: Though many of the thirty-six Frog Queens so far have been local girls, the pageant has never bothered to shut its doors to girls from elsewhere in the state, in part because its organizers have always prided themselves on grilling contestants about their knowledge of Frog City lore.

That this year's pageant comes down to two local girls doesn't say anything about Rayne's feelings toward outsiders, but it does guarantee that the winner will already understand the high expectations, endless duties, and low pay that accompany the title. The first taste of the position's intensity comes when a contestant reads the contract she must sign to apply. Not surprisingly for festival pageantry, she may not marry or get pregnant or commit a felony over the course of her year (or have done so in any year before). But those terms are perhaps easier for a girl of seventeen to twenty-three to abide by than her commitment to "act in a ladylike manner at all times"; for someone newly on the cusp of adulthood, it must be a bit chilling to learn that she is prohibited from ever engaging in "profanity, drunkenness, rudeness, vulgar or suggestive dancing, [and] public displays of affection."

Should there exist such a clean-spoken, sober, and polite girl who dirty-dances neither in public nor in private, she must then agree to participate in events both local (from small-business ribbon-cuttings to the Agriculture Installation Banquet) and statewide, including at least ten other festivals (from Buggy to Cattle). Not surprisingly, everyone associated with the pageant tries to be clear from the get-go: Frog Queen isn't just a prize, it's a job. For girls who are already busy with school and part-time jobs—as both Chelsea and Jennifer are—it's no light commitment to give up four out of every five weekends for the foreseeable future.

So how much does this lifestyle-restricting, time-sucking title pay? Five hundred dollars. *For the year.* Queens in other states tend to earn one or two thousand dollars, which is still a small amount, but more than Frog and most of her Louisiana counterparts make. Better still, the five hundred dollars only gets paid if the girl completes all of the above duties *and* has made a good impression as she does so. At the end of the reign, Beta Sigma Phi, the civic organization that funds the pageant, votes whether to award the queen all or none of the money. So a Frog Queen could conceivably represent the festival well at, say, thirty events but then embarrass herself at one or two, and end up with nothing at all for her troubles, not even the crown, which legally belongs to the Chamber of Commerce and Agriculture.

Still, there is no doubt that Frog is one of the most rewarding titles in all of Louisiana. Some of its virtues are the same things that make it sound like work: While there are

towns that cover their queens' travel costs for only a few outside events, the Frog Queen is encouraged to attend dozens if
she's up for it, knowing that she will be reimbursed for festival-
related gas and mileage. And while there are festival queens
elsewhere who preside over a mere one or two local events all
year long, the Frog Queen is a fixture of Rayne life, raising
money for breast cancer at Project Pink, delivering food baskets to the poor at Thanksgiving, hiding eggs for the Easter
egg hunt, and more.

Frog makes sure its queen never misses out on the ultimate festival pageant: Queen of Queens. Just over 80 of the
130-plus festival queens compete in the weekend-long Queen
of Queens event held during the LAFF (Louisiana Association
of Fairs and Festivals) convention in Baton Rouge. By the time
a girl gets to Queen of Queens, she's already had a taste of
being the face of a town, enjoying the fun of travel, and making new friendships with all the other girls who've walked a
mile in her dyed-to-match shoes, so the chance to ramp up
this magic can feel impossibly alluring. One girl's reign is extended as the new face of not just her town but all of the towns,
crops, and industries in the state. Long as the odds of winning
are, for a girl who truly believes in the value of festivals, it's a
dream come true.

Even so, Queen of Queens plays second fiddle to the Mystick Krewe of Louisianians Mardi Gras held in Washington,
D.C. A massive four-day affair, with meetings between politi-
cos and industry titans by day, and cocktail parties and dinners
by night, D.C. Mardi Gras culminates in an eye-popping ball

so epic and grand that it's the hottest ticket on the entire Louisiana social calendar. The luckiest partygoers in the state dance and drink with timber barons, oil magnates, financiers, philanthropists, and rafts of senators and Congresspeople. (Not only Louisiana heavyweights show up: Past partiers included future Presidents Nixon and Johnson in their early years.) The fact that it all takes place in Washington instead of New Orleans makes it all the more impressive that just about every major figure in the state attends.

For a festival queen, nabbing an invitation to D.C. Mardi Gras feels like winning the lottery. Just fifty of the festivals in Louisiana *ever* get to send a queen to D.C.; most that do only send their queen in alternating years, because the number of queens invited annually is capped strictly at twenty-five. The fortunate few enjoy guided tours of Washington, visit with Congresspeople on Capitol Hill, attend all the fancy parties, and revel in their roles as guests of honor at the ball, where they make grand entrances in a parade that takes pageantry to a whole new level.

Yet perhaps the greatest appeal of being Frog Queen lies not in the big trips but in the small town. Ask anyone about Frog and you'll hear the same mantra repeated again and again: "Rayne treats its queens like real royalty." No matter where she comes from, the townsfolk know her name and welcome her like family. Schoolgirls beam at her as if she's Miley Cyrus come to visit. The local newspapers run her photo. Every organization wants her to come to their biggest event, and they think it a shame if she doesn't. As Chelsea put it earlier in the day, "Frog Queen is just *that* girl, in the best possible sense."

So which girl will be *that* girl? Opinions are mixed among the Visiting Queens. Crawfish has only been to a few pageants so far, but based on what she's seen, she gives the edge to Chelsea. Fur, a few seats away, has been to dozens of pageants and, based on past experience, had initially thought it might be Hope; now that it's down to this pair, though, she thinks the will of the crowd is clear: The crown is going onto Jennifer's head.

But it's all guesswork until the name of the runner-up rings out. When Jennifer is called forward as 1st Maid, the two girls unclasp hands, but Chelsea doesn't move a muscle for a moment; she doesn't smile or cover her mouth in the quintessential moment of pageant delight. She is simply too afraid to believe that it's true, afraid of what it might do to her to think she has won if she hasn't. She has already lost this title once in front of all these same people, and she can't yet believe that she hasn't lost again.

The only thought in her head is this: *I need them to actually say my name before I can move. I have to* hear *it.* And then she does: At last there is only one girl, only her. The Frog Queen.

What happens next is combustion: First the air is sucked from the room, and then it returns in explosive applause. Jennifer may have had more vocal fans to begin with, but Chelsea's fellow citizens cheer her on now as she covers her eyes and fresh tears fall. From the look on the faces of the Visiting Royalty, it is apparent that most of them, like Fur, have misread the signs.

But it is just this kind of drama, the chance or even *desire* to witness an upset, that gives a night like tonight its allure and promise. And so surprise gives way to applause as they rise to their feet to honor Chelsea with the first standing ovation of her Frog Queen life.

As the other contestants head into the back room to change into street clothes, relatives and friends rush to join Chelsea at the stage. It is her story now, her evening, her year. A hundred out-of-town girls line up to congratulate her, posing for pictures and bearing gifts from their festivals to welcome their newly crowned sister. I watch her through the throng, wondering where this experience will lead her—where she will let it lead. She sees me, the stranger who happened by at the lowest moment of her day, and she waves, calling out, "I won't need to Google a new line after all!"

Beautiful in her relief, she disappears from view, cut off by the flood of Mamarazzi. All that remains visible is her crown, a jeweled landscape where a faux emerald frog swims upward, elegant legs propelling it toward a sky lit by the endless flash-bursts of Chelsea's victory.

3

Where Queens Come From

In my childhood, watching pageants was an inviolate family ritual nurtured by my grandmother, a tough old bird who would never have admitted to loving something so frivolous. Grammy had sharp opinions about everything you can imagine, a firm demeanor that didn't entirely mask her sentimental side. These warring attributes were never more clearly on display than on those evenings my family gathered in the living room to watch pageants big enough to air on TV. Let the first contestant totter into view on heels tall as a serving spoon and Grammy was immobilized, though not at all quiet. She'd lead all of us in a raucous exchange of opinions: *That dress with no back is* shameful! *This girl looks mean, sure enough, but the one next to her, well, she seems* nice.

The best girls had a backstory, some detail announced in a voice-over or revealed in the interview portion, or even just inferred by Grammy and then accepted as fact. God bless any girl with a past illness or a dead parent—one detail like that and Grammy had someone to champion. She'd loudly mock the judges' taste when her new heroine ranked poorly, or nod with amen fervor if the girl did well. And once there was a Good Girl, well, that made the other girls Villainesses. (She was especially likely to affix this tag to blue-eyed blondes, whom she viewed as having too easy a route to the crown.) Should the Good Girl not make it to the final round, Grammy would mutter her disgust, say the whole thing was foolish, and make a big show of dressing for bed before the winner took her victory walk. But should a gal with just the right backstory win, my grandmother would have tears in her eyes.

She would have *loved* Chelsea. Chelsea had not one, not two, but *three* physical ailments to overcome: scoliosis, a painful condition that made her hips uneven; a serious grass allergy that, having gone undiagnosed for years, kept her ill on and off for all of junior high; and a deviated septum that not only badly restricted her breathing but made her feel so "gross" (her word) that in eighth grade she tore up every single photo of herself she could find.

She was also cripplingly shy, hardly the ideal starting point for a pageant winner. But it's true: As a child, there wasn't a trace of Little Miss Sunshine in her. She was precisely the kind of girl about whom people say, "She never said *boo.*" Chelsea could barely speak to anyone besides her parents and older brother; even when her own aunts came over, they couldn't get a word out of her, as if conversation was physically painful. When she was growing up, no one, and I mean *no one,* would ever have pictured her striding across a stage in a sparkling evening gown, waving to hundreds of people as their new queen. And yet here she was, because one thing she never lacked was determination. She'd pulled off the hat trick of earning all three of the town's big titles, but only by losing each one first (including her initial attempts at Frog Derby and Miss Rayne) and then coming back, anyway. Did I mention that Grammy would have loved her?

Of course, if you take the time to find it, *every* girl has an untold story. The night of Chelsea's win, the Rayne Civic Center is full of them, each compelling in its own way. Over there, Washington Catfish clowns around with visiting royalty who are unaware that she battled depression in her first year as a festival queen. Crawfish looks so carefree that you can't tell she has spent her teen years shuttling between homes—living sometimes with her father and sometimes her grandparents, but rarely with her mother, who travels for work all but a few months of the year—and working to help pay bills the whole time. And what of the petite blond Fur Queen slipping out the front door without congratulating Chelsea? If my grandmother were alive, she'd instantly dismiss the girl on looks alone and then use the queen's poor manners—leaving so soon!—as proof that she was right to do so. Except she'd be wrong.

While Chelsea finishes posing for queen photos, Lauren Naquin, the Louisiana Fur & Wildlife Festival Queen, is desperate to find a place to get a burger. Lauren has held four successive titles, so she has attended well over a hundred pageants and knows she should have stayed for the receiving line, but she thinks she can be forgiven for skipping out quickly tonight: It was that or pass out in a satin heap on the floor.

She barely made it through the pageant. Exhausted from a day that included a five-hour work shift and a hospital vigil before the three-hour extravaganza got under way, she had her endurance tested further by the too-late realization that she'd forgotten to eat anything. By the time the judges were deliberating, her head was swimming and she was fighting nausea. Worried about keeling over, she did all she could to get by; from beneath her seat, she produced her heavy wooden crown box and hauled it up onto her lap, then closed her eyes and rested her weary head, crown and all, upon its smooth surface until Chelsea's name was called.

Outside now, she takes deep breaths of the air, which is finally cooling down a bit, and throws her crown box into the backseat of her mom's car. She climbs in and tells her mom to find food—any place will do. Though Lauren is twenty-two and lives in an apartment with her grown brother Aaron, her mom has been driving her around to festival events a lot lately as a safety precaution. This summer, Lauren discovered that being a pretty girl with a fancy crown can come with a risk she had never imagined when she first considered running for a festival title: A stalker had fixated on her for an unsettling week.

That experience was disturbing enough that Lauren has her guard up these days. It's the first time in her life that she has ever needed to rein in her natural extroversion. A pint-sized pixie with dimples, Lauren was born under a Shirley Temple star. Growing up, she'd been the social antithesis of Chelsea, not a bit shy, and always in the thick of things, from dance team to the Catholic youth ministry at her church. Even so, she had to be talked into running for her hometown title, Breaux Bridge Crawfish Queen, because she was sure pageants were all rigged. When she won, she discovered she was a natural at festival promotion, and her path was set. The next year, she nabbed a second title, Shrimp Queen (in honor of her mom's seafood restaurant), and the year after that, Cattle (in honor of her farming grandparents). Much like Miss Rayne runs for Frog, a Cattle Queen gets a "bid" (a paid entry and guaranteed slot) to run for Fur Queen when she finishes her Cattle year. In January, Lauren won that, too. She's been a festival queen for her entire college career.

Tonight a fast-food hamburger helps settle her stomach, and her head stops buzzing, but this pit stop makes the long day even longer. It's after midnight before her mom drops Lauren off at her apartment. Already imagining falling directly into bed (she doesn't keep pillows on it for the express purpose of not needing to move stuff to sleep), she murmurs only the most minimal "good night," hoisting her crown box and slamming the door behind her. As her mom drives away, Lauren thinks: *I made it through another day.* And that's all she can ask for right now.

Come morning, Lauren hasn't gotten much sleep, but that's not so unusual these days. While Chelsea heads to work at a fancy denim store in the mall, Lauren heads to Southwest Hospital in Lafayette, where her sister nearly died last week. At fifteen, Abby Naquin underwent gastric surgery to deal with serious weight-related health problems. The surgery itself had gone well, but her recovery had been painful, her bandages still wetting with blood for days afterward. Lauren and her brother, Aaron, took turns visiting Abby at their childhood home in Breaux Bridge while their mom was at work. One night, as Lauren ran credit cards and tidied up dressing rooms in her job at Head to Toe Boutique, Aaron went by to check on Abby and found her lethargic. He summoned his mom, who tried to rouse Abby, but getting Abby up made her pass out completely. An ulcer, which had gone undetected in surgery, had ruptured and she was hemorrhaging inside. While Lauren closed up shop alone, unaware of the gravity of the scene a few towns away, her sister nearly died.

Ever since, Lauren has spent part of each day in the ICU at Southwest. She hates going there, hates the smell and sound and feel of the ward where Abby lies prone. Lauren wants to be the strong big sister, so she doesn't want to cry, but it's hard not to when she walks into the room and sees Abby. "She looks so ill, so very white, with this tube down her throat and all these machines hooked up to her." Lauren sighs, "It just *kills* me." But Abby is awake and visibly happy about the visit, at least until her wan smile gives way to a bout of coughing, which sets off the mechanical alarms on one of the machines (or maybe two—it's so loud, so nerve-rattling, that Lauren can't be sure how many units are sounding off). Lauren hates to say so, but it is almost a relief when her visit is over.

Chelsea's afternoon is just getting started. For the past

year, she's pulled eight- and nine-hour shifts selling hundred-dollar denim to trendy types at Buckle, a jeans shop in the Mall of Acadiana. Tiny thing that she is, she often has to wrestle simply to pull the stacks of embellished jeans from the display cubbies where they've been wedged by workers on previous shifts. It's a bill-payer, this job, that's all, and she has grown to hate it, especially when she has to work with Penny, a forty-something dressed like a teenager who treats the job as if it's a fashion career. Penny thinks Chelsea isn't serious enough about sales (she's right), and Chelsea's heard that Penny gripes about her whenever she's out of sight. Work has become such a drag that the highlight is break time, when Chelsea heads to the food court for a daily meal of a pretzel dog with cheese sauce and a Dr Pepper. Her routine is so predictable that the vendor prepares her order as soon as he sees her coming.

Today she brings her velvet crown box to the store and unveils her new prize right there amid the jeans. (She does not, however, offer to find it in another size for customers.) Penny makes a show of admiring the crown, effusive in her congratulations: "Oh, Chelsea! Now we have a Frog Queen among us!" But she can't resist tucking in a subtle jab: "I guess we won't be seeing much of you, will we?" Chelsea thinks, *No, ma'am, you won't,* but she doesn't engage, for she knows that Penny really will complain endlessly about all the weekend shifts the Frog Queen must miss for festival duties. But Chelsea doesn't care: The Frog title matters in a way that the job does not. As she replaces the lid on her box, Chelsea doesn't tell Penny or anyone else a little secret about how happy she is to have this crown: Last night, she slept in it.

As the week draws to a close, Lauren and her family celebrate Abby's sixteenth birthday, newly and profoundly aware of just how precious such a day is. But they don't all celebrate at the same time, and not just because the doctors won't allow five people into the room with Abby at once. They are a ruptured family, and even their shared focus on this tragedy cannot make them a unit again.

Last fall, Lauren's parents split after twenty-four years of marriage. One morning, after first attending Sunday services like always, her dad moved out without preamble or fanfare. He briefly moved back in a few weeks later, saying he would try again, only to leave for good over the holidays. "I had always been Daddy's little girl," Lauren says, "so it was all so strange. I wasn't playing sides at first, but then he wrote me a text message one day saying I didn't need him and he didn't need me and I should go on with my life." Most children of divorce are fought over, their loyalties much desired, with both parents wanting to remain equal in their affections. To be cast off like this—to be cut loose by text message— seemed so cold, so callous, Lauren didn't even think twice. "I just stopped talking to him."

When she started the new year by winning the Fur crown, it seemed a blessing to have so many duties to fulfill in places far from all the drama. In the months since then, "I've already traveled thirty times for Fur, wanting to do them justice," she tells me. "And I think I have. But I also freely admit that being a festival queen is the best distraction I could ask for."

Meanwhile, she and her dad have barely spoken, estrangement replacing familiarity as the norm, at least until Abby's near-death experience. The first time her father appeared at the ICU, Lauren recalls, "he hugged me tremendously hard, and started to make this big speech, and I was like, 'This is *not* the time.' " In the last week, he has called Lauren six or eight times, but only with updates on Abby, and they still do not meet outside the hospital. On the easiest days, she doesn't cross paths with him.

Today, though, they make nice as their visits to Abby overlap. But as relieved as Lauren is to mark one more year of Abby's life, it's not much of a birthday. The hospital won't allow flowers in the ICU, and there's no cake, either. One of their neighbors has handmade a sign—HAPPY SWEET 16!—which they've taped to the cool hospital wall. And they've added a few balloons to make the room look as cheery as possible, but no one feels especially festive as they visit Abby in pairs and trios over the course of the day. The only birthday melody Abby hears is mechanical, the beeps and whirs of the machines that make it possible for her to be there at all.

Lauren has to work tonight, and even then she won't be done with her duties—when she gets home, she needs to turn in her RSVPs for Cattle, Cotton, and Yam, each one coming fast on the heels of the one before. The next few months are by far the most crowded on the festival calendar, and it crosses her mind that she could just resign Fur instead of trying to keep up. Considering everything that has happened in the past nine months (a backstory even my grandmother couldn't have made up), this is a forgivable impulse. Lauren can just envision how much time would suddenly be free, how she might be able to catch up on her sleep if she had to balance out only hospital visits, work, and college, without all the weekend duties. But the idea flickers and fades almost as soon as she entertains it. In a year like this, the support of her fellow queens seems even more valuable. Sisters, real and Rhinestone, are precious and can't be lost.

Besides, there are just over four months left in her reign, and soon after that she will turn twenty-three, aging out of competition, so this really is her last lap. There's no need to hurry the end along, especially at this moment when everything else is so unsettled. She gets all her RSVPs sent off without further delay.

Twenty miles away, Chelsea returns her first RSVPs as well, not just for Cattle, but for Rice right after that. Her own festival is still over a week away, but she will barely have time to enjoy it before her Visiting Queen duties take over. "Anywhere the town needs me to go, I'll go," she says with unstudied earnestness. "Whatever they want, I'm there." Fresh and untested, she's still less focused on what the title can do for her than what she can do for it. "I just hope at the end of the year, when I give up the title, the Chamber of Commerce thinks I did a good job for them, for *Rayne*. If they don't, I'll feel just horrible."

At this moment, Lauren and Chelsea seem divided by where they stand in the stream of rhinestone time—one putting the finishing touches on her legacy, the other eager to start crafting hers from scratch. Neither of them has any idea how much they will have in common in the coming months as unpredictable turns force both to reexamine what it means to be queen. In the face of suddenly altered expectations and withering public opinion, Chelsea will learn what Lauren already knows: Sometimes winning is the easy part.

4

Hurricanes and Other Storms

Chelsea has been Frog Queen all of one week when she logs on to MySpace to find an unusual message. Brooke, the former Frog Queen who had been the one local judge at Chelsea's pageant, has sent her a friend request. Brooke is four years older than Chelsea, so while they both grew up in Rayne, they've never been schoolmates, never had the same friends. When Chelsea was coming into her own as Frog Derby Queen and Miss Rayne, Brooke was on the move, out of state at one point, and she's now in Shreveport, three hours away. They know each other in the way that any two people from the same small town do, especially people involved in festivals, but they've never actually been friends in either the real or virtual world. So when Chelsea clicks yes to add this new online friend, she is curious as to why the request has come now.

Brooke has reached out to her for reasons not entirely social: She has the reputation of the Frog Festival in mind. She takes it upon herself to warn Chelsea that the new Frog Queen is being flamed on the Voy boards, the online forums that serve as the epicenter of festival chatter. It's not just Chelsea being targeted, but Brooke, too, and the attacks boil down to this: Frog was rigged.

If you're a festival queen in Louisiana, you face two main threats this time of year: that a hurricane will cancel your festival and that the Voy boards will make you wish you didn't have a festival to preside over in the first place. More festivals are held and more queens crowned from mid-summer through mid-fall than at any other time, and the potential for terrible weather—from simple rain to tropical storms and worse—has for decades been accepted as part of the bargain. But the risk of being flamed online at Voy.com is a more recent plague, a factor queens have faced only over the last four or five years. There is, of course, no real comparison in scale and depth between terrible acts of nature and tidal waves of human gossip, but that doesn't mean a queen can't still feel battered by both.

Voy.com is a compendium of forums, a half dozen or so of its message boards focusing only on Louisiana pageants. One of these, the Positive Chat board, is just what it sounds like, a nice place where people congratulate new winners, invite queens to their events, and keep up on all the festival news. Its subhead reads, "Please refrain from making negative comments about contestants, festivals, or organizations," followed by a warning that the moderator will remove all such rude posts. This stands in sharp contrast to the morale-killing prominence of the site's evil twin sister, the Louisiana Pageant Tabloids board, the logo of which is a map of Louisiana adorned with

an off-kilter crown, above a black cat with blinking eyes and
the slogan: "Pageants are a drug and we are all addicted." Nobody seems to moderate the Tabloids board, and vicious posts
aren't just not removed, they attract dozens of responses, some
worse than the original.

Right now the Tabloids board is hot, and the target is
Chelsea. According to one user, Brooke is Chelsea's "best
friend," and, so the post goes, the two of them were once seen
"out drinking together"; this is a particularly vicious claim,
seeing that Brooke's sister was killed by a drunk driver and
Brooke has made drunk driving a personal platform as a result. (It is worth noting that the user didn't care *what* the underage girl was allegedly drinking, only *who* she was drinking
with.) Another poster says that that Ms. Cheryl and her co-
director had been heard talking trash about the out-of-town
contestants because they only wanted local girls. A third poster
gripes that it should have been first runner-up Jennifer's night
because she was the one who had already served the town so
well. No matter that the "best friend" was already in college
while Chelsea was still ripping up junior-high photos of herself; no worries that nearly as many non-Rayne girls have won
Frog as local girls over the years; no concern that Jennifer's
primary qualification for the job is having held a title Chelsea
held first. All that matters is a chance to say that the outcome
was rigged.

Theories abound as to who is most likely to post on the
Tabloids board. There is a widespread belief that many posters
are part of a cadre of indiscriminately pageant-obsessed women

who make it their jobs to know everything about anything related to all kinds of Louisiana pageants, of which there are four
varieties: festival (like Frog), civic (like Miss Rayne), scholarship
(Miss America and Miss USA), and glitz (the somewhat creepy
circuit where Jon-Benets of all ages fork over cash to vie for
meaningless crowns like Miss Super Cutie and Dreamland
Sweetie). Among the ranks of these crown-followers, you're
likely to find some of the same pushy pageant moms and grand-
mas who torment directors and judges everywhere. These are
not the nice Mamarazzi; these are women who really wish that
their daughters were in the big pageants, who wish they had
raised celebrities, not girls who end up losing titles like Swine
and Bear. Sometimes, I'm told, it is the girls themselves—
unsuccessful contestants or even current queens upset by a particular outcome—who post the nasty statements. Other posters
seem to just sit by their computers day after day waiting to stir
the pot after events they never even attended. This is all conjec-
ture, of course, because posters are not required to use their
own names or provide an e-mail address—or display any firm
grasp of the English language. It is remarkable how many
people obsessed with pageants cannot spell the word.

Brooke has decided to take matters into her own hands.
She is annoyed at having her integrity as a judge called into
question, and figures that the best way to prove the wisdom
of picking Chelsea is by making sure the new queen suc-
ceeds. To that end, Brooke offers to act as Chelsea's mentor.
Having held so many titles in her day, Brooke knows everything Chelsea doesn't: what forms need to be turned in

when, what kinds of dresses make the right and wrong impression, and how to prepare for the big winter push when D.C. Mardi Gras and Queen of Queens happen in rapid succession. It's a win-win situation: Chelsea becomes a better queen, which in turn shuts up Brooke's critics, all while watching out for the interests of Frog, hometown festival to both. Chelsea agrees.

One of Brooke's first pieces of advice for her new pupil is to steer clear of the Voy boards altogether for a while. Having overcome so much emotionally even to win, the last thing Chelsea needs is to read all the venomous posts, which would surely mess with her head. Brooke will tell Chelsea when things are being written about the Frog Queen, but not in great detail, and only, as Chelsea puts it, "on a need-to-know basis." The good news is that the Voy boards are premised on gossips having short attention spans. The flames around Chelsea's story will burn out quickly enough, which is bad news for someone else—the forum will heat back up when the new Cattle Queen is crowned in two weeks.

Six girls are willing to take that risk in the hope of joining Chelsea and Lauren in the sisterhood. Cattle is what's considered a "state" title, which means that it represents an industry for all of Louisiana, not just one town or parish. There are perhaps a dozen true state titles, but thirty or forty others are treated as such simply because of their prominence or because a specific industry's reach exceeds its host municipality.

(Because the frog-leg industry was once so powerful and its
festival still is, Frog gets treated like a state title in a way that
many other local titles—like Miss Roastin' with Rosie Barbe-
cue or Luling Boutte Fall Festival Queen—do not.) Holding
a state title means you get the most invitations; when, say,
Strawberry Ball limits the number of visiting queens to twenty,
state titles like Cattle are far more highly represented than
local ones. It also means that your festival is likely to be on the
coveted D.C. Mardi Gras invitation list. Any festival girl can
tell you that this is a D.C. year for the Cattle Queen.

Among the six competitors at Cattle, two girls stand out to
me because of an unusual coincidence: They're both from the
same small town, but *not* Abbeville, where the festival is held,
nor even a town in this parish. Brandy Matulich and Kristen
Hoover are both from LaPlace, a town over two hours away
on the far eastern side of the state. Considering that, if one of
them wins, she will have to commit to driving 130 miles every
time Abbeville needs her, why would either want this job? As
it turns out, both are past queens who have chosen Cattle
partly because it is a state title: Brandy to prove that she can
win a state crown again after being away from the system for
more than a year, and Kristen to prove she can win one at all.

Despite its small size, their hometown of LaPlace is a two-
crown town. It hosts both the St. John Parish Sugar Queen
and Miss Andouille, titles that reflect the town's twin claims to
fame: the sugarcane fields that line the flat route between the
elementary school and high school (whose dancers are the
Sugarettes), and its fresh-made sausages, which are available

from storefronts big and small in the "Andouille Capital of the World" (as proclaimed by enormous letters high on the public water tower). Both industries' queens are fixtures, so local girls grow up seeing Sugar and Andouille at all the town events. "When you're little in my town," says Kristen, "you look up to the queens. I said, 'Mom, I want to be one someday.' " Both girls got their chance: Kristen serving as St. John Sugar, and Brandy as Teen and then Miss Andouille.

If you formed your opinion of the town's young women based on these two, you'd think LaPlace is breeding supergirls. Brandy seemingly can't slow down. "Throughout school, I did pretty much everything I could get my hands on: science fair, social studies club, SADD, Beta Club, and dancing." When asked how she kept up, she pauses a moment, as if to suggest that this has never occurred to her. "I stayed busy. That's my thing." Those words could easily have come out of Kristen's mouth, too, as the energetic teen was active in church, on dance team and student council, and in the Beta Club.

As if activities weren't enough, both girls prided themselves on their academics. Kristen loves kids and long ago decided to work with children someday; in high school, she started planning for the major in psychology that would begin her path to an M.S. and then a Ph.D. No slouch herself, Brandy was in the gifted and talented program, where "if they thought you weren't getting challenged enough, you got an extra hour outside the curriculum to challenge you more." In some places, such academic focus would make a girl a nerd or an egghead, but on the festival circuit, it makes her perfect queen material; it just so happens that she's likely also to be comfortable in sequins and stilettos.

Despite their similar trajectories, the two girls don't really know each other. Brandy is twenty-two and Kristen nineteen, so they've never had classes together, and they weren't town queens in the same year. They are also separated by personality: Brandy is quiet, watchful. With her ancestors' Acadian roots manifest in her black hair, dark brown eyes, and olive complexion, she has an exotic look for these parts, a kind of beauty that somehow makes it harder to read her emotions or intentions at a glance. This can be aggravating for her, as "people might think I'm being stuck up, when I'm just listening."

In contrast, Kristen's emotions are perfectly clear: On her open face, anger looks like thunder and enthusiasm (her default setting) like sunshine. She is a friend-collector and innately, irrepressibly chatty. "I am not shy at all," she laughs. "I can talk to anyone. Started when I was a baby and I'm still like that." Her mother says that you can tell when Kristen's sick because it's the only time she's quiet.

They are also divided by experience. As Miss Andouille, Brandy competed at Queen of Queens and snagged a red Top 15 pin on her first try, an impressive accomplishment for a newcomer from a less-known festival. She kept the streak going the next year by winning her first state title, Yambilee Queen, and felt on top of the world—at least until she got to Queen of Queens, where she found herself under a microscope. It became clear that she was expected to make Top 15 again— and then she didn't.

That disappointment would be followed by another, one a lot of girls can relate to, whether or not they've ever worn a crown. Once out of high school, she no longer had the hours of dance practice to burn off calories, but she was eating the same amount as she had before. In college, her life became more sedentary, focused on her studies, so physical exercise was limited. She'd gained thirty pounds since her first crown, and while this made her more curvy and womanly, Brandy felt less healthy, less in control, not really who she wanted to be. When her Yam reign ended, she competed for Rice, and remembers, "I was very uncomfortable with my weight, and that showed. You have to have a level of confidence to do anything right, and I just didn't." After two wins, Rice was a loss, and just like that, she was off the festival circuit.

Rice was a year ago, and she has spent the months since focused on two things: studying for her classes at SLU Hammond and working nearly full-time at Raising Cane's, a chicken-fingers restaurant. Cane's, as she calls it, is a chain that started in Louisiana, and Brandy believes in the company wholeheartedly. She threw herself into work, putting in long hours of "dropping bird," slang for slinging chicken fingers into the fryer. Over time, Cane's gave her more responsibility, eventually making her one of the location's managers, despite her young age.

Recently, Brandy's also been busy threading her way through the terrain of a new relationship. She hadn't seriously dated anyone in the past few years until this summer when Juicy appeared. "I'm not a dater, but he contacted me through MySpace. He saw pictures of me with people I know and wanted to meet me. He messaged me a couple of times and I said, 'I don't have time to keep messaging, so just give me your number.'"

Juicy may have made the smartest play possible for a straight guy: He took Brandy to the *Sex and the City* movie because he knew she was dying to see it, and he was pretty much the only six-foot-four 280-pound dockworker in the theater. She returned the favor a month later by using her one day off to sit alone in the pouring rain while he played in a softball tournament, an act that caused another attendee to praise her for being such a good girlfriend. "I'm not a girlfriend," she'd protested, but the next day Juicy called and asked her to check her Facebook account. There was a request to confirm that she was in a relationship with him. She let the big lug sweat for fifteen minutes, then clicked "Accept," surely the most twenty-first-century method possible for formalizing a romance.

Juicy's interest in Brandy broke a cause-and-effect chain that Brandy thought was pretty fixed. "TV and movies show that you have to have a guy to be happy, but that you have to be skinny to get the guy." Ironically, at her thinnest, she was single, and only after gaining the weight did she meet Juicy; though she'd already begun Weight Watchers when he first approached her, she was still twenty-five pounds heavier than her goal at the time. Considering that he liked her body as it was, she might have stopped her regimen then and there, but Brandy is determined to persevere for the sake of her own long-term well-being and happiness. With her mom as a Weight Watcher buddy, Brandy is aiming not for skinny but for healthy (think Marilyn Monroe, not Kate Moss). As Cattle approaches, her efforts have paid off: She's lost fifteen pounds of the gained weight, a big difference for a girl her size. She feels revived, not with the body of the teen she once was, but of the young woman she now is.

Unlike Brandy, Kristen doesn't worry about her weight that much. Kristen is five-foot-one and weighs 145 pounds, which a height-weight chart might label as overweight. But if you meet her, what you see is a vibrant sturdiness combined with the physical ease of a dancer, which she has been all her life. The only time her weight has ever come into question is when she considered trying out for a slot on the Golden Girls, the dance team for the LSU marching band. She talked to a current Golden Girl about her chances and was told that she would have to lose at least forty pounds. For her height, she could only be a Golden Girl at 100 to 105 pounds, and once selected, she would face weigh-ins at every practice. If she varied from her approved weight by more than two pounds, she would get one warning before being kicked out. "I said, 'No, ma'am. I can't do that.' But what I shoulda said was, 'I don't even *want* to.'" She found the squad's ideal weight offensive and the idea of two-pound "flexibility" just stupid. "I mean, that's water weight!"

That sentiment is not uncommon in the festival system. To be a festival queen, there is no height-weight chart except for the one a girl sets for herself. There are queens the size of linebackers and others who appear wraithlike, girls just tall enough to go on the big rides at Disneyland and others who have to duck through doorways. It's not just body type that doesn't conform to one neat image; there are queens with eyeglasses, problem skin, and braces—surface details that matter less to judges than the glow of the girl within.

Even so, state titles like Cattle are the ones most likely to attract girls who have perfected their looks as much as their skills, and Kristen knows this. "I told my mom, 'There are hard-core girls who do this pageant—this will only be my second ever, and I'm just a newbie. I don't know if I can be that ready.'" It's not just that she's never held a state title; she's never *won* a pageant at all. At the one parish pageant she entered, for St. John Sugar, she came in second. But just weeks later, the girl who came in first captured the statewide Queen Sugar title. In a classic employment of the should-the-winner-not-be-able-to-fulfill-her-duties clause, Kristen was elevated to St. John Sugar Queen after all, enjoying almost a full year's reign.

Now she wants to experience what it's like to be a state queen before she starts her senior year. Kristen compared all the festivals, and then chose the one with a backstory that really touched her. "I knew Cattle had a lot of support from the community, but then I read that during [the floods of] Hurricane Rita, the farmers went head-deep in water to save their cattle. How can you not support that? That's when I knew."

So both girls have something to prove, personal goals that will be met by a win. They also share something else: potential criticism over whether they should be competing for Cattle at all. "The only negativity I've really received about competing," says Brandy, "is that I'm perceived as a 'Crown

Chaser' for competing in more than one pageant a year. But it's not about the crown at all. It's about the recognition and attention you bring to your festival and how that can be used to promote and advertise."

Not surprisingly, Kristen agrees. "I don't think you have to be from that area to be a good representative. If you put your heart and soul into it, and you know and promote that industry, which is *your job,* why can't you be from somewhere else? Just being from a place doesn't mean you'll know any-thing about its industry."

To prove that they will indeed be able to speak well for this festival hours away, both girls are studying up on cattle during every free moment—or not free, as the case may be. Brandy is preparing even while working her shift as a manager at Cane's; when she's hefting fifty-pound boxes out of the back of a truck on delivery day, there's no way for her coworkers to tell that she's also thinking about the role of the beef industry in Louisiana. Kristen has been on the computer constantly, gath-ering information that she then studies while on the elliptical machine. (She sighs, "I love that machine but it *hurts*.") She's been spending time with a cute boy named Chance, whose family raises cattle; whenever they have a moment to spend together, he quizzes her about things like the twenty breeds of cows in Louisiana.

With the pageant less than two weeks away, the girls can see the end in sight. But to live in Louisiana is to live with the unexpected. Whether you believe in God the Father or Mother Nature, there's no denying that huge celestial forces batter this low-lying country regularly, which is not the same as saying predictably. While Kristen memorizes cuts of beef and Brandy buffs up on Abbeville lore, Hurricane Gustav smashes into Cuba and then, instead of calling it a day, sets off on a collision course for Louisiana.

Because the Frog Festival usually occurs two weeks after its pageant, Chelsea has not yet had a chance to preside over the Frog Races or attend Frog Mass or ride in the Grand Parade like she's always imagined. And now she may not get to. Frog is slated to begin in four days, and all the news stations can talk about is Gustav. The third hurricane of a mean season that has already smacked Louisiana with Tropical Storm Fay, Gustav is headline-worthy not only for its strength and size, but also because it invokes Katrina and the destruction of New Orleans. Covering Gustav becomes a way of tapping into all of that once again. The broadcast media love a narrative, which in this case seems to be "Will New Orleans be hit again so soon?" But anyone who reads the storm maps on the Web can see that the Big Easy isn't the main target of this storm—unless it changes course, Gustav is going to move west and inland, right over Rayne and Abbeville and a hundred other small towns that don't merit CNN ticker coverage.

Suddenly, festival plans are secondary. Chelsea's family packs up and heads west to Galveston, well beyond Gustav's reach, to stay with relatives. When they arrive, the vacation playground of the Texas coast seems completely disconnected from what is happening at home. "Everyone's at the beach, swimming and playing, lying out in their bathing suits," Chelsea says. "No one's even talking about the storm."

Meanwhile, Brandy, her brothers, and her mom are heading north to Arkansas. Listening to storm news on the car radio, Brandy has an embarrassing realization: In the middle of a hurricane, she has brought her Cattle pageant dress with her. "What am I thinking? What does a dress matter if I go back and there's no town there?"

At this very moment, Kristen is driving toward Memphis in what feels like a clown car, stuffed as it is with a brother, mother, grandmother, and two dogs. They are among nearly two million people fleeing the storm in one of the largest evacuations in American history.

The state is in full disaster mode: The Mississippi River is closed to Gulf traffic; in low-lying Plaquemines Parish, unmoored boats are being sunk to avoid causing damage, while a highway has been cut off by the hurried creation of a new sand levee; voluntary and mandatory evacuation orders have gone out from parish to parish; and oil operations in the Gulf are at a near-complete halt, the eerily quiet platforms now somber giants bobbing in the sea.

Gustav comes ashore packing 115-mile-an-hour winds (dipping just into the Category 2 realm). Its winds do in fact reach New Orleans, but it directs most of its anger toward the central coastline and inward from there, with flooding and tornadoes as its handmaids. All day, the news headlines will read that New Orleans has been spared, but that note of cheer misses the debris raining down in the streets of Baton Rouge; the mall roof collapsing in Alexandria; the trailer thrown from its base in Evangeline Parish, killing two of its occupants. For many thousands of Louisianians, New Orleans's relative escape is little comfort at this moment.

Fur Queen Lauren is one of those people. For her, it is a frightening day. As the daylight hours wane, she and her brothers, Blake and Aaron, wait in their childhood home in Breaux Bridge for Gustav to roll in; when it does, they lose power and are left sitting in the dark house at the storm's mercy overnight. They have stayed in town because Abby is still in the ICU, and their parents have been allowed to ride out the storm by her hospital bed in Lafayette. Though Lauren and her brothers are technically adults, a storm this size makes them feel like little children as they find themselves unable to close their wide eyes and sleep. Only the roof of the one-story brick bungalow lies between them and the rain and a wind that shrieks relentlessly. The terrifying sound ramps up their fears of what they can't see: How is the hospital holding up? Does it still have power? Will Abby be okay? It takes hours for the worst of the storm to pass.

Kristen is also missing a parent right now; her father, Steven, is flying around the state surveying damage in his job with Entergy, the utility company. Crisis is not really when her mom, Lisa, is at her best, so Kristen takes charge of the family. First, they drive to Memphis, where the hotel they've booked is so dirty that no one wants to sit down. There are no sheets on the bed, there are piles of ashes in the ashtrays, and even the phone is broken, missing the pan where the numbers should be. Eventually, it is too much, and after milling around Memphis with other displaced Louisianians, they decide to return home as the storm wanes.

It's the middle of the night by the time they arrive in LaPlace, and the power is out all over town. Only the head-lights of Kristen's car illuminate the way, as she strains for glimpses of the familiar. Things look different without all the streetlights and glowing storefronts, and debris has changed the shadowy contours. As she describes it, "I've lived here my whole life and I'm like, 'Where am I? Am I even on my street?' "

Once safely back at home, the Hoovers have no lights, no a/c. Lisa can barely breathe in the face of the stifling humid-ity, and makes it her first order of business to open all the windows. But it doesn't help—to her horror, not the faintest breeze stirs even so. It's up to Kristen to explain the situation to her mom: The house feels airless because they're still *sealed in*—Dad boarded up all the windows before he left. (With no power inside or outside, Lisa hadn't even questioned how dark things looked.) These conditions won't do, and so they pile back into the car before dawn, heading 260 miles north to Jackson, Mississippi, in search of a hotel with air, light, and even sheets.

When sunlight returns that morning, the first to know that things will be all right is Lauren, who is awakened by her mother coming through the door. "Everyone's okay?" Lauren asks, surprised that the worst is over already. Her mother assures her that Abby and both parents are no worse for wear. She has only come home for a shower and, miraculously, the water works just fine.

Kristen and Brandy alike return to LaPlace (Kristen for the second time) to find their town, and their own homes in particular, pretty much intact. The yards need a little clean-up, and in the Hoovers' case, someone has to pull all those boards off the windows. Rayne, too, has come through the storm almost untouched, at least compared to after Hurricane Lili, which wiped out entire neighborhoods in 2002. Chelsea has never lived anywhere else, so it is a relief to come home and find her town whole.

As Rayne is largely unaffected, the Frog Board gets back to work on its festival, even as some locals wonder whether it would be better to postpone it to a later date. One phone call from across the state takes the decision away from the board: The owners of the Mitchell Brothers Carnival point out that much of I-10, the highway leading to town, is still closed. With no road for Mitchell Brothers trucks to get into Rayne, there can be no carnival, and a festival without a carnival is nothing but an open-air concert without enough snacks. If storm clean-up isn't itself enough to depress the numbers for Frog, surely having no rides or games or food will. And so the news release goes out: Frog is rescheduled for November—the latest it has ever been. Only time will tell just how costly this decision might be.

Chelsea can't help it: She's disappointed. When she was Frog Derby Queen, Hurricane Katrina led to Frog being postponed by a month. It's as if she brings doom to her own festival. But in the short term, the board's decision to move the date turns out to be a very wise call. On the day Frog would have started, no one is thinking about outdoor parties; all eyes are on Gustav's ugly younger brother Ike, which turns into a Category 4 storm at sea.

A case of sibling rivalry on a massive scale, Ike apparently needs to outdo Gustav, its maximum sustained winds hitting 145 miles per hour, and it, too, wants a shot at Louisiana. Over the next few days, as it creeps closer to the U.S., it becomes clear that Texas will get the biggest blow, but that Louisiana communities from the mid-coast west will all get a taste of Ike's fury. After a week of Ike-watching, the outlook gets even grimmer on the border of Texas in tiny Cameron, home to the Fur Festival. Though Lauren's actual hometown of Breaux Bridge has been spared by Gustav, her festival town won't get off so easy. It sits directly in line to take Ike's full brunt—and it does.

People die, entire neighborhoods are shredded, buildings fall, landmarks disappear. Eighteen hundred of the town's houses—home to 80 percent of the population—are badly damaged or entirely destroyed, along with the post office, bank, grocery store, churches, and schools. It's so bad that FEMA, after initially offering money for newly homeless residents who have no insurance, will soon prohibit the rebuilding of property in 80 percent of Cameron Parish, leaving many residents with literally no place to call home again. The next time that Lauren sees the parish she represents, it won't look anything like what she remembers. While Chelsea may be a queen without a festival for the moment, Lauren now reigns over a festival without a town.

Yet, inevitably, life is a forward-looking business. The skies clear, the earth spins, and those not completely laid low by disaster turn their eyes to the possibility of better news and brighter days. Wall Street went back to work within days of the September 11 attacks, even as the ruins continued to smoke. China focused on Olympic festivities just three months after seventy thousand of its citizens were killed by one of the deadliest earthquakes of all time. And so, too, Louisiana, rocked by $10 billion in damage spread across more than half its parishes, picks back up what remains of festival season, and the Cattle pageant opens its doors right on time. Kristen and Brandy will get their chance after all.

5

A Win and a Loss

Chelsea arrives with seconds to spare. She has a thing about being perfectly punctual for any event in which she is representing Rayne (and could pretty much care less the rest of the time), but she's let her mom drive her to Abbeville High School for the Cattle pageant tonight and they got horribly lost on the way. (It could've been worse: Kristen and her mom have gotten lost within Abbeville's five square miles *twice* today.) Cutting it so close makes Chelsea crazy because tonight is her first royal duty as Frog Queen. One of the very first instructions she received from her mentor, Brooke, was, "Get your ass to Cattle!" Not only is this pageant a contracted event for a Frog Queen, it's one of the most prominent titles in the state, so tonight provides high visibility for Visiting Queens. It's especially important for Chelsea: She must seize every available opportunity to implore audiences to come to Frog on its newly rescheduled November date.

As Chelsea hurries inside to freshen up, she is alerted to some bad news by an older woman in the restroom: There is a dark, terribly placed stain creeping down the back of her gown. "Is it that time of the month?" the stranger croons, not especially sweetly. (The answer is no, which doesn't help explain the stain's origins.) Chelsea could die: Tonight the Visiting Queens aren't allowed to wear their mantles and trains, so there will be no easy way to hide the hideous mystery blob. As the pageant starts, all she can do is sidle quickly into her seat and then find a way to keep her backside facing away from every single person she meets for the rest of the evening.

Sitting a few seats away, Lauren is a jumble of emotions. She cannot help but let her eyes drift to the row of royal banners hanging above the stage. In most festivals, each queen makes a wall banner depicting her reign, to be kept by the festival itself. Banners from past years, sometimes decades, are the signature decoration of many pageants. Tonight banners are hung at rafter height, fluttering slightly and glowing in the spotlight. For Cattle's contestants, the banners represent a club they'd like to join; for little girls down front, they are the flags of a glittering future. For the Moo Sisters, the dozen past Cattle Queens in attendance, they're reminders of the mark each queen made, proof that she left a legacy.

One banner features the name of Chelsea's mentor, "Brooke Ashley Henry," written in elegant cursive above a field of grazing cows. Another banner mirrors the Cattle Queen's crown, which boasts the chocolate-and-white face of a heifer rendered in gemstones. A few banners away, a more subtle sheath with gold fleur-de-lis on maroon velvet bears the name "Lauren Elizabeth Naquin." Made by her mother, it should be the icon of good memories for Lauren, but the banner is heavy with complicated associations. It marks not only the night two years ago when she was crowned Cattle Queen, but also the night she gave up her crown a year later. Her still-married parents had started bickering during her farewell, and her mom snapped at her dad, who left abruptly. As Lauren and her boyfriend drove to Chili's after the pageant, she said of her father, "He's gonna leave my mom." Lauren's boyfriend told her she was crazy, and she consoled herself that it really was a ridiculous notion. That was Saturday night. On Sunday morning, her father left.

She would never have been able to predict the terrible year that followed, capped the week before last by the devastation of the parish she represents. For days, she has been trying to get ahold of Vicki Little, her director. Landlines are down, and even texting hasn't worked. Completely cut off from the festival and town she represents, she watched the news every day, horrified at the images of wreckage. After she was finally reduced to sending Ms. Vicki an e-mail, Lauren's words of worry seem to have disappeared into a cybervoid, ineffectual. And now all anyone at Cattle wants to know is whether her festival is still on for January or not.

She tries to distract herself tonight by examining the six girls who want to become a Moo Sister. As the contestants are introduced, they make a striking visual—tall and short, fair and dark, plump and skinny, clad in gowns of five different colors: black, red, orange, green, and white. Lauren recognizes Hope right away, wearing the same black gown she lost

Frog in, looking even more poised and commanding tonight. Kristen is one of the two girls in white, both wearing sleeveless gowns, and she hopes that this duplication won't hurt her. She'd bought a new blue gown—which would have stood out more—but hadn't gotten it altered before the hurricane. This older dress sets off the darkness of her hair and eyes, but her skin is pale enough that her bare white arms do not stand out especially against the gown. Lauren, who fits queens for gowns all the time at her boutique, thinks the dress isn't a plus for Kristen.

The six contestants smile bright smiles as the judges consider them, and their shared energy helps draws focus from the incongruous background: a faux brick storefront featuring an enormous glass window bearing the initially incomprehensible legend "stnalP s'kinhsuM" and "woR dikS." If it were possible to stand on the other side of the glass, you'd find yourself looking through the window of "Mushnik's Plants" on "Skid Row," which is to say that the pageant stage is doing double duty as the set of a high-school musical. The Cattle Queen will be crowned in the Little Shop of Horrors.

As the girls leave the stage, Lauren and Chelsea consider their future peers. Lauren competed against Brandy for Yam two years ago and lost, so she knows Brandy can deliver. Remarkably, Chelsea, too, has competed against Brandy. At the same Rice pageant last year where Brandy had felt so awkward about her body, Chelsea had attempted to compensate for her first Frog loss by competing for the festival title next closest to home—and lost again. But Chelsea remembers little of that evening and, tonight, Brandy registers as only vaguely familiar. Chelsea's main impression is that Brandy is "just gorgeous, I mean absolutely beautiful." Based on the contestants' initial introductions, neither Chelsea nor Lauren will be surprised if Brandy wins.

One by one, the contestants are called to return for the onstage question, filing past the seated current Cattle court. The Petite Cattle Queen swings her feet, which do not reach the floor, while the Teen Queen, nearly swallowed up in the pink ruffles that pile up around her like a rose-petal barricade, carefully tracks the contestants' moves. Brandy speaks thoughtfully, but perhaps a bit too softly for an onstage interview. There is the slightest tremor in her voice, and she knows it. When she finishes, she hopes that her content will carry more weight than her delivery. It is Hope who does best in the onstage question, her voice clear and confident, her answer smart and solid. The Visiting Queens look at one another, nods of approval indicating that they're impressed—they know a good answer when they hear one.

Kristen, last to be questioned, cannot tell how either of her main rivals has done as she waits backstage. Alone in the greenroom, she tries not to let herself get too intimidated. "Of course you get all nervous. I see all these other girls who won their titles and won them outright, when I didn't, but I know there's no telling: You get one set of judges and they'll pick this girl, and a different set of judges and they'd pick another girl entirely." She's pretty sure that she came off well during the closed-door interviews earlier in the day, but she's aware how quickly a good impression can go sour. "You know Miss Teen South Carolina—I do *not* want to be her, the girl who gets onstage and freaks out and just stands there. What if the question's really complicated and I can't answer?"

Finally, she is called out onstage, a silk-clad jumble of confidence and trepidation. The other five girls, all of whom now know the question, stand onstage smiling at her, ripe with knowledge and curiosity. She can barely hear the question, something about what influence a Cattle Queen can have on the lives of farmers in a difficult economy, and she panics for a moment. Her brown eyes look away from the judges, scanning the stage floor as if reading a map, a way to buy herself time to come up with something; later she will have no idea what she said. When the contestants all walk offstage, she grabs the pageant director. "Did I make *any* sense?" The director says she doesn't know—she was busy behind the scenes, not watching the pageant at that moment. From where she sits, Chelsea thinks that Kristen is done for.

So when Hope comes in third—again—and Brandy comes in second, Kristen's win is nearly as big a surprise as Chelsea's had been a few weeks before, which only proves that there is a certain kind of memory loss that comes over pageant-goers in Louisiana. Despite knowing that a good interview with the judges offstage is the single biggest deciding factor in choosing a queen, audience members cannot help but get caught up in what they see, forming firm opinions about who should win based on a walk in an evening gown and a two-minute question-and-answer exchange. Only at the end of nights like this one, when a girl like Kristen seemingly comes out of the blue to take the crown, does memory of the actual scoring process return, with both Lauren and Chelsea telling me, "She must have won at interview."

Not everyone agrees. The hurricanes may be out to sea, but the Voy boards haven't gone anywhere. Even while Kristen is taking pictures with her new Rhinestone Sisters like Chelsea, while her mom snaps photos to add to the scrapbooks of Kristen's accomplishments and her dad discovers (through a discreet pair of radio headphones) that her victory has just been matched by LSU's football team, the Voy boards have made Kristen their target.

By the time the Hoovers head home from Outback Steakhouse, where they celebrate her win, the online rumor mill is grinding away. Kristen, so it goes, was coached by one of the judges. In Louisiana a pageant coach is typically an older woman or experienced festival participant giving a girl advice and helping her prepare for an upcoming contest. For a contestant to be judged by her own coach is an obvious conflict of interest, but it's no easy feat to pull off even if you wish to cheat: For this to happen, girl and coach alike would have to lie to the pageant director and keep everyone mum, including all their friends and family and all their family's friends and their families—not easy in the everybody-knows-your-name festival world. It is telling that the first Voy post about this alleged fixed outcome is framed as a question: "Is it true that . . ." As the claim is feverishly debated, it becomes increasingly clear that some of the most vociferous posters aren't sure which judge was the alleged fixer, and some aren't clear even who *Kristen* is. When she crawls into bed that night, she falls asleep unaware that people are already calling her a cheat.

Brandy hears the rigging rumor before she even leaves the high school, but she shrugs it off. To be honest, she's relieved to have done so well on her first return, which feels surprisingly like an opportunity. Cattle has served as a warm-up for Brandy, a way of getting back in the game: She leaves Abbeville feeling enough renewed confidence to compete in two weeks for Queen Cotton, a title that she's been secretly pining for all along.

Fourteen days later, Brandy's confidence is being tested by the unusual conditions placed on contestants by the Cotton Festival. Unlike Cattle or Frog, in which the queen's pageant and her festival are held on separate weekends, Cotton crowns its royalty during the festival proper. The would-be queens must spend not only the day of the pageant together, but that night as well. They fill their time shuttling between a Cotton board member's cottage, which serves as their barracks, and the Civic Center, where both interviews and pageant are conducted. They must ride to and from all these events together by bus, instead of traveling there with family or friends. When the pageant wraps up, they must bunk together overnight in the cottage, in part to ensure that the full roster of competitors will show up to ride in the next day's parade, after which they are finally released. The notion is that this will promote solidarity and camaraderie among the girls, some of which does end up on display; but the impossible-to-avoid truth is that opponents are forcibly made roommates.

Today the Cotton bus is full, with six contestants and the twenty Visiting Queens who have been invited to participate, and an undercurrent of tension pervades the bus ride, thickening the air with unspoken—or at least whispered—opinions about who deserves to win. There are three kinds of contestants, divided into pairs: local girls, who can stake claim to hometown loyalty and knowledge; former festival queens, whose Rhinestone Sisters would love to see them back in the mix; and girls who don't fall into either category, and as a result have not yet accumulated ardent supporters. In the local girl category, one of them has already served as Miss Ville Platte and is required to compete for Cotton, but she confides in the others that she is not thrilled to be here; her fellow local is Nicole Charlie, who has perhaps the best claim to the crown: This is her third year running for the title she truly wants. The two past festival queens are Brandy, ready to make the leap from foods to fibers, and Orelia Lawdins, a law student and former Meat Pie Queen.

In theory, any girl can win any pageant on any given day, but among this particular banner-and-crown set, the prevailing opinion is that this battle will come down to Nicole and Brandy. A coterie, which some bus riders have dubbed "Team Nicole," has formed around the local front-runner; including several current festival queens and another town titleholder, they are adamant that this will be Nicole's year, and they aren't alone. On the Voy boards, one headline reads: NICOLE CHARLIE!!! THIRD TIME'S A CHARM! NO ONE LOVES COTTON MORE.

Nicole isn't the only one with a cheering squad; Brandy has Queen Sugar pulling for her, as well as the outgoing Queen Cotton, her friend Amy, who had begged her to run in the first place. Lauren is in this camp, too, and though she didn't start the day out as Brandy's ally, she has become defensive of Brandy over the last few hours because she knows what it's like to be the outsider competing against a hometown girl. With conflicting camps crowding the bus, the girls are glad to arrive at the Civic Center, where they busy themselves straightening their suits and smoothing stray locks before meeting the judges.

The Northside Civic Center in Ville Platte puts on few airs. Boasting a sturdy, inexpressive facade one might think of as airplane hangar chic, the three-hundred-seat arena is the kind of place where the people who fill it make all the difference between sterile and inviting. When the contestants see the judges lined up waiting for them, *inviting* isn't the first word that comes to Brandy's mind. The three-person panel is composed of a couple—no less than the president of the Louisiana Association of Fairs and Festivals (LAFF) and his wife—and an older pageant director. That's just about the toughest panel combination you can face, as far as Brandy is concerned, because couples tend to vote as a bloc and because the more experienced directors ask the toughest questions. The good news for her is that all three judges are so well versed in the statewide festival system that this panel will likely be a challenge for the least experienced competitors, and it offers no home-field advantage for either of the local girls. Brandy faces a level playing field, and she might even have an advantage.

The LAFF president grills the girls with state-related questions, including "On a scale of one to ten, how would you rate Louisiana's education system?" That's a loaded question, which can easily be answered too negatively or too positively; it's a perfect way to see how a queen handles a tough issue on the spot, not just in words but in demeanor. The solo judge makes sure the girls are cotton-savvy, asking them to name the greatest threats to crop production, a list known in Ville Platte as "The Seven Evils of Cotton." You can't just wing your answer here—guessing at seven natural factors, for instance, will only get you halfway. You'd have to have done your homework to know that the list is (appropriately) a blend of the natural and the man-made: silk, rayon, nylon, flood, drought, boll weevil, and bollworm.

After a very late lunch of—what else?—gumbo and a mere hour to prepare for the actual pageant, the girls take their places in the Civic Center. They sit onstage in white resin chairs for the duration of the event, the only light in the auditorium illuminating their reactions for the audience to see. Behind them, the back wall is hung with a pastel fairy-tale scene, which lends the stage the air of a prom photo backdrop. The judges sit on the floor of the auditorium, and when it is time for the evening gown competition, the girls walk down

out of the light to stand before the panel, hoping to be flat-
tered by whatever residual glow spills onto them from the
stage lights. It is unnerving to model so close to the judges and
at eye level—the girls can actually follow a judge's gaze wandering critically from detail to detail. Nicole, in powder blue,
with a thigh-high slit that seemingly doubles the length of her
already-long legs, appears to be the one to beat. Orelia is radiant in white, but beyond being possessed of a winning smile,
modeling isn't her thing. And Brandy, though she radiates
beauty and poise, is sure that she's too close to the judges, who
can see that her shimmering green silk gown is just-this-much
too long. When the modeling is over, it is a relief for the girls
to be released from such close scrutiny.

The onstage question probes them about how they would
use their Queen Cotton status in the aftermath of a hurricane.
This is not a rhetorical question. The combination of Tropical
Storm Fay with Hurricanes Gustav and Ike has cost Louisiana
cotton $136 million in the past two months. Vice Chairman of
the National Cotton Council Jay Hardwick appeared before a
Senate committee and explained the ensuing cycle of loss:
eighty thousand destroyed acres means a loss of more than half
the state's crop value for the year, which leads to limited operations and budget cuts at gins, warehouses, and grain elevators,
which in turn means lost jobs and lower income to rural communities. Since this year's Queen Cotton will serve as a public
ambassador for this newly wounded industry, as well as attend
agricultural council meetings in this rebuilding year, each girl
knows her answer to this question has to count.

Brandy doesn't want to make promises no one would find plausible, so she speaks instead of how she would use this platform to make it clear that the farmers have local support in the community. For a moment, she thinks she has nailed it—right until Orelia answers with confidence and impeccable logic: "I'd vote." The former Meat Pie Queen goes on to explain that it's the people who get elected who can make the most real difference for the farmers. Brandy's immediate thought is, *Man, I hope she sucked at interview.* When the girls are once again seated, the easy Brandy-versus-Nicole contest has been transformed into a three-person race.

Brandy finds herself within moments of either being Chelsea—the girl who had to lose first to win after all—or Hope, the queen who keeps trying and cannot find her way back. And the personal stakes couldn't feel more profound. One of the ultimate fantasies for many festival queens is to be crowned queen by a dear friend; such an outcome is not unheard of, but it's less common than many girls would like. Brandy knows girls who have enjoyed this particular alignment of stars and have shared that bond ever since. She wants that kind of experience with Amy, and wants it badly.

Amy's slender fingers hold the crown aloft, the stage lights bouncing off its jeweled ivory cotton blossom and emerald-green leaves. Brandy knows that if that crown comes to rest on any head but her own, there is just no way she will be able to mask the depth of her disappointment. But then the emcee calls her name and she doesn't have to. Her friend at her side, a hundred camera flashes capturing this moment, the new

Queen Cotton is awash in relief and thrill and accomplishment all at once. Not winning Cattle feels like the best thing that could have happened. The lost year is gone; Brandy is back.

But hers is a joy that must be tempered. Because of the Cotton rules, she now has to get back on the bus with the very same girls she has just beaten and return to the cottage. Not allowed to go out to eat with her family or celebrate with friends, she instead must engage in the first public relations duty of her reign: being a graciously understated winner, watching out for the feelings of those she has defeated.

Before the bus leaves, the camps have hardened further. Lauren overhears Team Nicole saying that Brandy doesn't really care about this title, that she won't travel enough to make Cotton look good. It's ironic, because if Brandy had won Cattle, as many expected, it might have been fair to accuse her of not being invested in her title, but now that she's earned the crown that matters most, she's under fire as a pretender, a sham. Lauren wants to say something like, "Get over it," but it's not her fight.

When the bus pulls up at the Cotton cottage, one girl is not on board. Rules or no rules, Nicole has gone to McDonald's with the director of another pageant so that she may grieve her loss away from the others. She is not present when Team Nicole loudly discusses Brandy's not deserving to win within earshot of Brandy herself. The new Queen Cotton knows how frustrating and hurtful this loss must be to Nicole after three tries, and she wants to be understanding, but she also wants to just be happy about her achievement, which she feels she earned fair and square. She'd rather be out to dinner with people who love her, not here, in a strange house, hearing how much her win bothers her roommates. She hasn't had her crown for two hours and already it weighs on her.

It won't be long before the Voy board take up the cry: Why does a girl from halfway across the state need to compete for Cotton, anyway? What is she, a Crown Chaser? All Brandy can do now is spend the year proving the critics wrong and the judges right. In the Voy board age, that's all *any* queen can do. The best rebuke to online gossips is to appear again and again, event by event, doing your job, talking up your festival, and making sure that what people see with their own eyes exceeds what is whispered online.

Kristen understands this. By the time Brandy is crowned, Kristen's friends have told her not only about the first Cattle-rigging post, but about all the variations that have since been added. She shrugs it off. "It's just people trying to start stuff. They don't know what they're talking about. They even have a story that my Momma was a former Cattle queen, which anyone can tell you isn't true at all." And as far as she's concerned, that's the end of that.

"Ya know what? I'm such a non-drama girl that if they wanna talk about me, they're wasting their time."

To some extent, the Voy board users know that she's right. One reason the online posts can get so nasty is that no matter what their authors say, no matter how many rumors they bring squalling into life, they are powerless when it counts most. By the end of this month, more than three-quarters of the girls who will be competing for Queen of Queens will have already been crowned, and the Voy boards will have cast the deciding vote exactly zero times. The truth is this: The yawp of the poster is the cry of the defeated. Like Lauren before them, Chelsea, Kristen, and Brandy are all queens now, and there isn't a damn thing the Voy boards can do about it.

WEEKEND WARRIORS

*Do you sit at home and
let your crown get full of dust,
or do you put on your crown
and let it get full of festival dirt?*

> —*Chelsea Richard,
> 2008 Miss Rayne Frog Festival Queen*

6

Field of Queens

In the parking lot of the Super 1 grocery store in Abbeville, the rising sun hits a row of float trailers lined up side by side in the predawn. Waiting for the Grand Parade of the Cattle Festival later today, they sit largely empty for now, casting shadows across the blacktop of the otherwise vacant lot. The sun is not yet high enough in the sky to make the gold foil fringe sparkle or to brighten the paint jobs that distinguish this one's patriotic theme and that one's Mardi Gras mural. The wooden face of God peers impassively off the end of one float, ignored by the plaster-of-Paris masked man fronting the next. The only occupants of the floats at this early hour are an elderly man in a VFW cap and his grandson, who together are drilling bolts and cinching ropes to ensure that no one topples from a perch mid-parade.

While most of Abbeville sleeps, Chelsea is already on the road headed here from Rayne, a half hour away, her black Mustang gliding past the Super 1 and down Rodeo Road. That's RO-dee-oh not roh-DAY-oh, and it's a Road, not a

Drive, which is to say that this is country: The horses here are flesh and blood, not simply handbag logos.

Eight A.M. and the sun is creeping ever upward as Chelsea pulls the Mustang into a grass parking space at the Ag Barn. In an enclosed cattle yard, other newly arrived festival queens and a few parents mill about waiting for the morning's duties. One of the signature aspects of a festival queen's job is to be open to fulfilling whatever traditional tasks other festivals ask of her—shucking oysters, say, or racing crawfish. As your own festival's reputation attends you, you must step up to any plate, and Chelsea aims to do just that, though this morning she's not really feeling it. Checking her cell phone for messages from Jace, her boyfriend, and finding none, she straightens her shoulders and gets out of her car. Pausing only to don her jewel-studded banner, she heads for the fenced-in enclosure, not sure exactly what awaits her.

Already in the yard is a family of local farmers, the Menards, who have brought two of their cattle to meet the queens. Dad Mike and mom Paula each have an animal in hand, Paula leading a fawn-colored calf named Buddy and Mike keeping a firm grip on a chocolate-and-white bull named Mr. Puzzles. Mike explains that the tradition for festival queens is to milk cows at this event, but not today: The cows in Abbeville have been stressed by the back-to-back hurricanes, so milk production is down. Nobody wants to subject their already-taxed animals to the inexperienced hands of fifteen or so well-intended queens, even in the name of tradition, so this year the cows will be on the receiving end of the exchange instead. The queens will bottle-feed Buddy, an enthusiastic calf who looks ready to consume the entire container at a gulp, and some of the queens look a little nervous.

The first to step forward is Kristen, happily in charge as the new Cattle Queen. This is her first royal responsibility of the day, though not her last, not by a long shot, with festivities stretching into the night of the sixteen-hour tour before her. While Chelsea is clad in her version of casual wear—a snug ivory sweater and cute flats—and most of the other queens wear jeans and sneakers, Kristen is dressed in goofy festival at-tire: a black-and-white cow-print dress. She stands in the wet field, her feet in flip-flops made of the same material as her dress; her footwear is perfect for a Cattle Festival, if less ideal for walking through morning dew (much less a potential cow-patty minefield). But she doesn't care about getting damp and dirty—this is what makes Kristen Kristen. She's a no-fuss girl with enthusiasm for life, and hers is a festival that emphasizes down-home fun. If ever there was a perfect fit between a queen and the ethos of her festival, this is it.

As Paula hands her the bottle, which is the size of a quart of milk, Kristen adjusts her crown—all of the queens, even out here in this field, keep their crowns on—and points out that she comes from a town known for sugar, not cattle, so this will be an entirely new experience. Nonetheless, she dives right in, while her mother, wearing a Cattle Festival T-shirt, snaps pic-tures of Kristen talking to Buddy. Once their queen has set the stage, the other members of the Cattle court, known in Abbeville as the Herd, get in place to take their turns.

The youngest of the Herd is the Baby Cattle Queen, a two-year-old with a huge bow atop silky locks. She brings to mind a china doll come to life wearing overalls instead of crinolines. The bottle is nearly as long as her arms, and she must hold on to it with both hands in order to not drop it. But she backs away every time Buddy tries to get a taste of the nipple, and her mother can't convince her that it'll be okay. The mother exhorts her, "Feed her like you'd feed Sissy," inadvertently comparing her youngest child, still an infant, to livestock. This does the trick, and Buddy finally latches on.

If a toddler can feed Buddy, anyone can, and the rest of the queens line up for their turns. Because it is so early, and so many queens must travel hours to get to Abbeville, the turnout is small, with perhaps a dozen visiting royals joining the Herd for field events. (Double that number will arrive later, for Kristen's Queens' Luncheon.) Chelsea hangs back a little, keeping close to her Teen Queen, Kelsey Primeaux, who has also turned out to represent Frog. Chelsea isn't quite herself today, which she quietly attributes to her grass allergy. Being allergic to grass might complicate the life of a girl constantly attending outdoor events, but something in her eyes—a look that says her mind is not on the hungry bovine pal before us—makes me think that isn't really the issue.

When the other queens have all finished, Chelsea and Kelsey finally step forward to feed Buddy, who is now on his third or fourth bottle. Chelsea's arms are stiff as she holds the plastic container out to the eager calf, and her posture doesn't soften at all until she tries to steady Buddy by placing one hand on the patch of copper fur atop his head. This contact seems to ground both of them, queen as much as calf, and she relaxes a little.

But this is only the first task of the day. Mr. Puzzles, a sweet name for a large beast kept in check only because an iron ring has been plugged through his nose, is not there merely for show. The queens are meant to *ride him*. Mike assures them that Mr. Puzzles is a gentle animal; he jokes that the bull will probably only throw a *few* of them. No one moves toward the bull until, again, Kristen takes charge, letting the eldest Menard boy, Kyle, help her mount Mr. Puzzles. She not only keeps her poise, she changes position a few times, even stretching out lengthwise in the pose of a daydreamer who just happens to be nestled on bullhorns instead of pillows. The hardest trick is not keeping her cool or maintaining her balance but finding a ladylike way to get on and off the bull while wearing a short, flared skirt.

Once Kristen is down, she goes the extra mile, grabbing Mr. Puzzles' lead rope and pulling his enormous face close for a kiss. Though it's an air kiss, it's just close enough to his dripping nose to make several of the queens a little queasy, their cries of "Yuck!" mingling with applause at her daring. Chelsea has a different take entirely, thinking about what that iron ring must feel like for Mr. Puzzles, and murmurs softly, "I feel bad for his nose."

Just as the visiting queens get ready to take their turns aboard the bull, he pees, a loud and steaming stream that merits a unified chorus of "Ewwww!" from his audience. The

Rayne girls are quick to point out that they are not spared this kind of hazard just because they handle frogs; not only do frogs pee unexpectedly, they do so while the queens are holding them in their hands for the endless girl-with-toad photos demanded by the local press. Chelsea explains that a *smart* girl knows to hold her frog away from her whenever the cameras are off.

As girl after girl climbs aboard Mr. Puzzles for pictures, Mike gently teases Chelsea, somehow intuitively tapping into the fact that she is reluctant. "Don't tell me yer scared!" he ribs her, and she takes no offense, but she still grabs Kelsey for a little safety in numbers atop the bull. They settle in, not an inch of space between them, to pose for their pictures, as Kyle quietly leads Mr. Puzzles by the nose for a short walk of just a few heavy steps.

Kyle is the real deal. All of seventeen, he is already an experienced bull-raiser who shows in 4-H competitions and won the Grand Champion prize at the LSU AgFest, which attracted thousands of young farmers a few months back. But he sure doesn't look like any of the farm boys I grew up with in rural Maine. With half his hair dyed red, the top of one ear pierced, a black T-shirt with an ironic slogan (*Let's Get Ready to Stumble!*), and camouflage cargo pants, he would look equally at home at a rock club in the East Village as here in this pen with livestock. It's a trippy vision: Lollapalooza meets Miss America on Old MacDonald's Farm.

The surreal aspect is ramped up when his cell phone fills the cattle yard with song. Pulling his phone from a hip holster, he answers with a bark of, "I'm in a field with the queens." When the person on the other end apparently expresses confusion at that remark—and you have to admit, it would sound pretty random out of context—he just repeats himself, louder and more emphatically, "the *queens,*" as if that explains everything.

Having ridden Mr. Puzzles, Chelsea appears a little less reluctant now, and she kneels down to stroke his forehead where the creamy white fur is dappled among the brown. Mr. Puzzles reacts to her touch as if she is an old friend; he closes his eyes and nestles his full head into her lap, which melts her heart. "I like cows now," she says with a tender laugh, stroking his sleepy face.

Moments later, as things are breaking up and girls start heading to their cars, Mr. Puzzles turns back into a bull. It's not his fault, really: Little Jabian—the youngest Menard— perhaps feeling bored and left out of the fun, has begun what he calls "surfing" behind the bull. By this, I mean he pulls Mr. Puzzles' lead beneath the bull and out the tail side, holding on to the strap with both hands while leaning backward. He resembles not a surfer but a water-skier, with bull as motorboat. Light as a feather, Jabian—who looks like a young Haley Joel Osment—first glides along the grass, easy with laughter, but then Mr. Puzzles picks up the pace, pulling the boy onto his belly and dragging him across the cattle yard and then out the front gate, which is open for departing royalty.

Holding crowns and scattering like leaves blown by the wind, the queens let Mr. Puzzles race by, with Mike hard in pursuit. Mike tells Jabian to let go and his son obeys, but there is still the matter of catching the bull, so Mike dives for the rope himself and lets Mr. Puzzles drag him flat on his back out into the gravel yard. Dirt flies into his face, his ball cap is flung wide, and his body bounces hard all the way, but he knows that eventually the weight of a grown man will be more than Mr. Puzzles feels up to pulling. Mike laughs as he is dragged, a bravado perhaps meant to keep the girls calm, until at last he has worn down the beast. Mr. Puzzles stands in place, mighty chest heaving, nose running a stream. Field duties are over.

Up next is the Queens' Reception in the local Chevrolet dealership. As Chelsea pulls up, the lot is near full, the sunny day attracting as many car shoppers as visiting royalty and their guests. A roaming salesman starts to head toward the new arrival until he sees her crown and deflates a little; he goes back to strolling among shiny new pickups. Checking her cell phone again with a grimace, she discovers there's still no message from Jace; though she's been trying to reach him since last night, she's come to realize that she's dating someone with a bad case of Romantic Attention Deficit Disorder. She can hardly be surprised anymore, but she doesn't have to like it.

Inside the dealership, Cattle royalty and their families, as well as Visiting Queens and theirs, chat in small clusters, outnumbering the seating options, which consist of a few metal folding chairs and a comfy couch typically used by customers while an earnest-sounding agent disappears to talk to a manager. As a stream of late-arriving queens join them, the girls do what Rhinestone Sisters always do: fall into conversation immediately, catching up on the others' lives and travels, chatting as if they've been friends forever. A handful lean against a huge gunmetal Silverado so neatly aligned with the food-serving table that the truck bed seems like an extension of the buffet.

The mayor of Abbeville is here with his pretty wife, both of them tan and dressed with a casual Western flair. Local kids all grown up, they greet the visiting queens and help put them at ease. "Local" hardly covers it in the mayor's case: Mark Piazza has never lived more than seven blocks from the house where his family lived when he was born. Suzanne Piazza has a fondness for the girls before her, with whom she shares a crowned history—at their age, she was Miss Abbeville.

Chelsea shakes hands with the mayor and dutifully tells him that Frog's date has changed to a new weekend, but after that she doesn't linger. By doing her field work, she's put in a good showing for her festival today and can keep her appearance at the luncheon brief. One of her aunts is getting married and the wedding starts in ninety minutes, which leaves Chelsea barely enough time to hurry home, ditch her jeans and crown, and slip into the outfit she has picked for the occasion. The silky one-shoulder floral dress features a twirly skirt that would be just perfect for dancing with Jace at the reception, except that he finally texts her to say he isn't coming after all. Her royal-duty smile dissolves and hardens into a mask of irritation as she leaves the luncheon, but nobody inside notices her departure; today all eyes are focused on the Cattle Queen.

While her invited guests chat with one another between displays of fat silver rims, Kristen flits about the Chevrolet showroom easily greeting strangers, a life force of enthusiasm. Her dark eyes are bright, and she exudes so much energy that, at only five-foot-two, she still seems a large person. My mind cannot help but leap months ahead, to Queen of Queens, and wonder whether this might be the kind of girl who will impress the judges.

It's been a few short weeks since her crowning, but it seems as if Kristen's been queen forever. She's already made television and radio appearances, attended the Sunday beef cook-off, opened the festival, and appeared at the formal festival banquet, even while commuting ninety minutes each way to school in Baton Rouge, which started three weeks ago. And she's hardly broken a sweat. She laughs, a smoker's laugh without the smoking, admitting, "I've *always* been busy. Now I just have to do time management during the week and queen stuff on the weekend."

To this mix, she's also cemented her relationship with Chance, he of the soap opera name. Because she's had bad luck with boys, she didn't jump on that wagon immediately. "My junior year of high school, my boyfriend cheated on me, so I go slow now." But with the pageant behind her, she and Chance have made things official. Though he isn't at the luncheon, it's no reflection on his interest—he escorted her through the festival crowds all last night, a chivalry Chelsea would kill for.

Denise Mire, the Queens' Coordinator, comes by urging everyone to eat. In southern Louisiana, food is god and you simply submit to it. Louisianians are not prissy about eating, embracing as they do specialties like crawfish, whose heads you snap off so you can suck out the goodness. And then there's cracklins, thick chunks of pork skin and fat deep-fried in lard. They taste heavenly (*Pig-fried pig, amen!*) even as they ooze sin—a little thrilling, a little dirty, the kind of thing you just *know* you'll pay for later. Nowhere else in the world is this the diet of pageant girls.

Kristen barely has time to eat. Her mom, Lisa, rushes her out the door for the Grand Parade, one of the highlights of any queen's duties. This starts a wave of departing queens, crowns disappearing among rows of enormous trucks, leaving the showroom to feel vastly empty in their wake, no sparkle remaining save sunlight off hubcaps.

While Chelsea is headed into the air-conditioned comfort of a country club for her aunt's wedding, Kristen could use a little cool air. For her ride atop the local royalty float in the Grand Parade, she has chosen to wear black—an idea that now seems less a good thing as the mercury unexpectedly creeps toward ninety. Her choice has a logic: The dress is composed of two layers, a black lace overlay atop an ivory base, which makes it an elegantly subtle companion piece to the cow-print dress she wore earlier—same palette, less moo.

But now she must wear it, in direct unobstructed sunlight, for the two and a half hours it will take to complete the four-mile-long parade route that begins back on Rodeo Road.

At the other end of the route, her mom and dad camp out on the steps of Abbeville's courthouse, a two-story building with fat white columns and a lovely balcony. Cattle is not the only big event over which the imposing courthouse presides. You might think it would be enough for a town of fewer than twelve thousand to host one major festival, but Abbeville is home to several. In Abbeville, history and tradition favor the Cattle Festival, but it's upstaged in pomp and circumstance by the Giant Omelette Festival, which involves a Mass that ends in a procession of costumed knights called Chevaliers. The Chevaliers carry more than five thousand eggs through these same streets to a specially designed twelve-foot skillet perched over a wood fire, where chefs gather with boat paddles firmly in hand to stir the bounty. But as there is no Omelette Queen, Kristen reigns alone and supreme in this town.

Those of us at this end of the route won't be seeing her anytime soon, as the first fire trucks of the parade are just now coming into view. On either side of Charity Street, crowds are lined up on the baking sidewalks as the parade's two hundred entries creep along slowly: high-school bands in syncopated swagger, soldiers keeping step in steely ranks, revelers in clown face and Holstein print, and a range of dignitaries whose offices are denoted by headgear ranging from cowboy hats to tiaras. Though this parade is considerably larger than its many counterparts at other festivals, the paradegoers here care less about its size or who sits atop which float. All they want is swag.

In the homeland of Mardi Gras, it is no surprise that people at a parade expect, at the very least, to be showered with beads. It's not as if beads are in short supply; countless vending carts roll by hung with waterfalls of colored strands, hippie doorways on wheels. But choosing your own beads—worse, *paying* for them—misses the promise of a parade. If you're going to leave the climate-controlled comfort of your own home to stand on hot concrete for hours, you want free goodies in return. And it isn't only children running, hands out, toward the loot-bearing floats in search of shiny necklaces, whistles, plastic toys, or the true grail of parades: candy. The crowd here isn't picky— fireballs, root beer barrels, Bazooka gum—candy is candy, all of it meriting screams of approval.

Children's dance troupes earn cheers as well. Tiny girls, some perhaps just three years removed from crawling, now skip and swirl along in sequin-studded bodysuits with bright skirts. Named for regional industries, there's a set of adorable Sugar Cubes and a Tabasco-themed cadre called Hot Stuff. Mostly girls of color, with beaded braids swinging in step and dark skin glistening in the heat, they light up the route with their plucky presence even as they themselves flag. A pickup truck follows behind one ensemble, scooping up dancers just as they reach their physical limits. As the truck pulls away, its bed full of exhausted miniature heroines, the girls receive an- other round of applause, but they are too busy toweling off and taking noisy hits off juice boxes to notice.

As the Cattle royalty float rolls into sight, Lisa and Steven Hoover, seated in camp chairs on the steps of the courthouse, finally get a glimpse of their daughter. Despite the two-hour wait and the heat that Lisa's umbrella cannot entirely keep at bay, their enthusiasm is high. Kristen looks beautiful in the top tier of the green-and-gold float next to the Cattle King, an army major general three times her age. Her dangling earrings act like sun-catchers, as brilliant as her crown. In her black-gloved hand, she holds a queen's traditional scepter, and she looks every bit the part. Those of us seated now rise in honor of Kristen and her fellow royals, ready for the tradition that is the annual highlight of the parade: the chocolate milk toast.

Back in 1949, the big event was known as the Dairy Festival, as the local milk products industry was very extensive. According to Mayor Piazza, the dairies slowly began to go out of business, even as the cattle industry thrived. By 1979, Abbeville was deeply invested in its primary local festival, which had grown from one day to three, and was so popular that one year President Truman attended. Instead of letting the festival die out with the dairy industry, Abbeville rechristened it to keep up with the changing times. Drinking milk at the apex of the parade is a way of nodding back to the festival's origins; it's chocolate milk because, well, chocolate is fun.

When the royal float arrives in front of the courthouse, the entire parade stops. Everyone's eyes turn to the queen and king, who rise from their thrones and receive glasses, which they hoist in honor of Abbeville. It's a liquid benediction for the parade, which will wind down soon after they resume their seats and roll on their way. For her first year in charge, Ms. Denise has decided to improve on that tradition. She has ordered commemorative goblets for the king and queen and included glasses for the younger set as well, thinking how much nicer the experience will be for them if they, too, get to salute the town. She can just see it: a half dozen royals, young and old, goblets held aloft reflecting the sunlight—the perfect crowning moment for the parade.

At least that's what's supposed to happen.

This year there's a new driver behind the wheel of the truck hauling the royals. He knows where the route begins and where it ends, but apparently nobody has mentioned what happens in between. As spectators rise for the toast and Ms. Denise stands ready to hand off the goblets, the float doesn't slow down. It continues rolling, past Kristen's parents, turning the corner to head past the courthouse to the end of the route. On the float, in the street, on the steps of the court-house, people are shouting, "Stop! Stop the truck!" But the parade is noisy and their pleas are lost in the din, the driver unable to distinguish one crowd sound from another. At this precise moment the parade emcee's sound system goes out, so he cannot project his plea, either. Even visual cues don't get the driver's attention: Spectators stretch out their hands in use-less mime as if to slow the vehicle's motion, but to an un-trained eye, it just looks like more revelers grasping for beads in the way that revelers always do. The float keeps on trucking.

Ms. Denise, just over five feet tall and gifted with unflap-
pable energy, has nowhere to set the chocolate milk down
and no time to waste, for she knows she has to save the day.
Running down the sidewalk, full glasses aloft and sloshing,
she screams at the driver. Perhaps it is the frantic shree of her
voice that finally pierces whatever fog he is in, or maybe he is
startled to look out the window and see a tiny figure running
alongside the truck waving dairy products at him. Whatever it
is, it does the trick, and the float finally rolls to a halt.

It is remarkable how little chocolate milk has been spilled
in her sprint, and so, with beads of sweat on her forehead providing her with a crown of her own, she proudly delivers the
near-full glasses to their intended recipients intact. Honestly,
the toast itself feels somewhat anticlimactic comparatively:
The running of the goblets will be all anyone remembers.

And then the float lurches back into action, the royalty disappearing around the corner to finish the route. Paradegoers
begin to disperse, fanning themselves and talking about the
heat, while a few determined children run freely through the
now-empty thoroughfare, eyes scanning sweltering asphalt for
glimmers of plastic or glass that might reveal an unclaimed
candy or one more string of beads. A line forms at the window of Miss Beulah's Creole Kitchen for juicy po'boys served
with a heaping handful of napkins to catch the drippings, as a
balloon vendor rolls by for the last time.

When Kristen comes back into view, she has cast aside
queenly poses and polish, less concerned with looks than
comfort. There she is, walking down the main drag shoeless, a

behavior so very Kristen but one her mom still cannot believe. Kristen laughs off the concern and focuses on a more pressing issue: Having already completed her third royal duty of the day (with more to come), she's ready to eat. Even a Cattle Queen can't live on chocolate milk alone.

7

Walk This Way

Often, in the peak of Louisiana festival season, a single week-end is plump with royal activity. Just as the Cattle Festival winds down in Vermilion Parish, the Honey Bee Festival is crowning a new queen in Livingston Parish, while the Rice Festival is paying tribute to its outgoing queen in a gala ball down in Acadia Parish. A girl can't be in three places at once, but Chelsea doesn't have to think hard about which festival to favor after the wedding reception ends: Not only is Rice the festival that gave birth to Frog, the Rice Ball is formal, which means she will finally get her shot at walking in full regalia. This is, literally, no small thing.

Chelsea's mantle is shaped like peacock feathers in full display, its eight segments fanning out above her head and be-yond her shoulders, adding five or six inches to her height and doubling her width. The train has a top layer of heavy forest-green velvet, upon which a frog scene is embroidered in a mosaic of fabric, thread, and gemstones. The unseen un-derside of the train is lined with a heavy plastic so that, at least in theory, the train will drag smoothly as it stretches out eight or ten feet behind her. Add crown and scepter and the ensemble is a serious burden. She still remembers the first time she ever saw a Frog Festival queen in her regalia, and thought, *How can she possibly walk in that?* More than a decade later, tonight is her chance to find out.

Twenty-five Miss Queens have chosen, like Chelsea, to head for Crowley, the Acadia Parish seat and home of Rice. As they arrive from all points, late light throws shadows across the flat of the earth along Route 13. The main route into Crowley, 13 is a slim ribbon of highway through rice fields wet and vast, the town's gold. White grosbecks on skinny legs walk tip-talon across muddy earth, graceful as queens on heels.

Crowley is a town that wears its agricultural identity on its architectural sleeve. There's a Rice Hotel, with an enormous *Jetsons*-era sign, and a Rice Theatre, where gospel concertgoers and Cajun-music audiences stream through glass doors beneath an elegantly nostalgic pink-and-green art deco facade. In this town where two hundred buildings are listed on the Register of National Historic Places, Main Street is outlined by tall double-globe street lamps that illuminate brick-fronted businesses that speak of an era when building materials were heavy, enduring.

Crowley's charms fade a bit on Mill Street, where I arrive to meet Chelsea, who has invited me to see her first formal walk. Multiple stories of grim white siding capped by tin roofs, the rice mills look like nothing so much as oversized Erector sets for giant toddlers, with metal ladders and chutes and conveyors sticking into and out of every building. The International Rice Festival Building, where the visiting queens have begun to gather, is an aesthetic improvement comparatively. Though it appears flat in relation to the mills, the Festival Building actually boasts high ceilings, its front double-paned windows rising a story and a half behind the portico-cum-carport entryway. Young women in jewel-studded gowns hurry through the entrance as we arrive, their presence dressing up the scene.

Crowley first crowned a Rice Queen in 1927, but she and her successor were Rice *Carnival* queens, and the tradition didn't stick, dying out after only two years. It would be a decade before the idea of a National Rice Festival would take hold—and truly seize the city's and state's imagination. The organizers didn't aim small: They blanketed newspapers nationwide with press releases and photos of Crowley rice harvests, and even made short film reels to show before movies. This early version of a media saturation strategy worked perfectly—thirty-five thousand people turned out for the 1937 festival. Attendees enjoyed not only a parade, but a double public wedding planned just for the event. And, of course, a girl was crowned the very first National Rice Festival Queen. When the festival was re-branded as the *International* Rice Festival, so, too, the queen's title changed. For a while, even foreign rice queens were invited to compete.

Crowley isn't the only town ardent about its rice. There's been a Rice Festival in Winnie, Texas, for some forty years, a week-long fete with horse shows, karaoke, nightly street dances, and a queen whose win entitles her to the use of a golf cart for getting from event to event. The Weiner, Arkansas, festival includes an all-rice luncheon and a parade honoring the state Rice Queen, chosen in part for her rice recipe. (This year's winner made Taco Rice Casserole.) And this is not just a Southern comfort. From Deer River, Minnesota, to Fall River Mills, California, rice draws big crowds. And if celebrating this glutenous wonder in the United States isn't enough, you can groove to a rice beat in France or Ghana or Thailand, where remote hilltown maidens, in headdresses as dramatic as any crown, take turns on a two-story-tall swing to celebrate the rice harvest.

When it comes to having a prestigious title, though, Crowley's Rice Queen rules above her similarly titled peers, thanks both to longevity and the fullness of her slate of duties. To earn this honor, she must first endure the same socially awkward ritual as Cotton: Rice requires contestants to spend the entire weekend together, including after the winner is announced.

Because Rice is the festival where the Frog Derby started, and the Frog Festival grew out of that, Rice is considered the next best thing to a hometown festival for Rayne girls. Chelsea competed in Rice immediately after her first Frog loss, but when she arrived for the shared weekend, she found herself unprepared for the thick air of such an environment, having previously experienced only Rayne pageants, where would-be queens mingle just for the day. At Rice, some of the girls were just like the ones she'd encountered at home, friendly peers willing to lend a hand, or in Chelsea's case, help curl the back of her hair, a feat she's never been able to master herself. But there was also at least one Crown Chaser with a serious competitive streak, and for whom sisterhood was out of the question. That girl kept her clothes in locked cases so no one could spy on the outfits she had brought, even as she perused her competitors' wardrobes as a sort of fashion reconnaissance; she bragged that she had brought so many options that she could avoid duplicating colors or materials worn by the other girls, and would thus stand out. Brandy was competing that year, too, and she remembers the girl well. "I was always used to girls acting more like, 'Can I borrow this lipstick?' or 'I like those earrings.' It's so bad to say, but we were all hoping it would be *anybody else*. Why would she have to be so mean?"

Tonight, Chelsea feels safely removed from that kind of drama, concerned only with the impression she will make. She's getting butterflies at the very thought of her first walk. Since most festival events require girls to wear only crown and banner, the few balls and pageants that do specify train and mantle are big deals. For years, Chelsea has watched other queens make their way solemnly down center aisles—trains stretching yards behind them, mantles framing their beautiful faces like gossamer wings—and she always knew that someday she'd do that, too. But now the night is here and she's thinking about the reality of this scenario: Fifteen pounds of regalia is roughly 16 percent of her body weight, and she's never tried wearing it all at once before—much less while walking in four-inch platform heels.

It would help if she had someone to lend a hand while she gets ready, but her mom can't make it tonight and Chelsea just heard from Jace that he isn't coming. In their two years together, it has become a well-established pattern that he will promise to show up for something that matters to her and then find an excuse not to at the last minute. Even if she is no longer surprised, the disappointment still stings.

An announcer asks the crowd of several hundred to take their seats. Though many among them are farmers, they are dressed to the nines, nearly all in black, defying notions of what country looks like. Once we are seated in rows of long white tables, the lights go down and a spotlight is trained on the Grand March of festival royalty. A military honor guard takes up station on either side of the center aisle, standing silent and impassive as the terra-cotta sentinels in the tombs of China. The outgoing king and queen make their entrance and then climb the stairs to the dais, where the queen sits in a fan-backed rattan throne that just begs for the return of Joan Collins. With the current royalty ensconced, all eyes are trained on the double doors at the back of the auditorium for the procession of visiting royals to begin.

As the queens enter the Hall, it is easy to understand the appeal of this tradition. With crowns and scepters catching the spotlight's glow, they are moving light-bearers. With faces at once young and regal, they carry history with them in every step. To see them is to see all their predecessors, the ones who walked this same aisle last year and ten years ago and twenty more before that. At my table of ten, every single person is the parent, sibling, relative, or friend of a past festival queen. For those gathered here tonight, these queens are their native culture, the grand myth of a people sewn into velvet and silk, underlined in rhinestones.

As thrilling as it must be for the girls to carry such a role, it is not always effortless. Some of them glide up the aisle as if wearing mantles made of chiffon or clouds, while others go slowly and with so much focus, one imagines them uttering silent prayers that they will not trip on their own hems. Miss Evangeline Oil & Gas discovers an engineering problem: Already a tall girl, she has added high heels and a yard-high mantle to her stature, the sum total of which renders her so amazon-like that she cannot pass through the door at full height. To enter the ball, she must duck, not easy on stilettos and in a straight-line evening gown. To pull it off, she imitates a giraffe, knees kissing while ankles fan out, dipping her crown-heavy head and lowering her mantle just enough to scoot under, and then manages to keep going, never loosening her grip on her scepter.

Queen after queen goes by until the final one—Chelsea—comes into view. She takes a deep breath, straightens her shoulders, and enters the ball. She takes tiny steps, testing the weight and drag of the green velvet train that stretches behind her. The pragmatic detail of the plastic underside lining, while ostensibly making the fabric glide along more elegantly, comes with a downside: As the train swooshes noisily up the aisle, it sounds exactly as you'd expect—like a heavy plastic sack being dragged across a cement floor. Even so, Chelsea is doing beautifully:

her smile bright, her posture perfect, a girl unimpaired by her elegant load.

Until the turn.

She has almost made it, has arrived at the front of the auditorium and nodded in royal greeting at the seated queen and now needs only to find her way to her assigned chair. There's the rub. The queens must make a U-turn at this point, reversing course and heading for the back of the room, this time passing on the far side of the honor guard. Chelsea tries to turn gracefully and finds her train, which is over six feet wide, resistant. She gamely forges on, even as one corner of the train catches on the boot of a soldier. If it were you or I standing there, our footwork impeding the progress of a queen, the natural impulse would be to solve the problem by simply lifting the foot in question out of the way. But an honor guardsman isn't made an honor guardsman for his flexibility. Impassive, immobile precision being the hallmark of duty, the soldier neither glances down at his boot nor moves it.

Every step farther away from the guard pulls more of Chelsea's train over his foot, first swallowing the toe and then the tongue and then heading upward toward the ankle. Soon enough the rippling train stops slithering along completely, settling into a tight green coil as it consumes the entire boot, a gem-studded python gorging on leather. The soldier does not move and the fat snake of fabric does not move, and so Chelsea, finally, can move no farther. She is a prisoner of velvet.

Fortunately, this is Louisiana, and some in the audience have experienced train emergencies before. Several women, elegant in black, rush from their tables like ladies-in-waiting and wordlessly set to work, deftly strong-arming the material until it relinquishes its grasp. Throwing the cloth well clear of any other footwear, the volunteers set Chelsea free on her way and return, without comment, to their tables.

This, as it turns out, is the high-water mark for excitement. The two dozen queens in attendance are seated in a grid of folding chairs, with a yard of empty space between each. This setup was intended as a way of making space for all the regalia. But its effect is to keep the girls well isolated, unable to visit with their Rhinestone Sisters, islands in a silk archipelago. For the next two hours, they will sit stiffly in place, balancing plates of thick pork gumbo on their laps, listening to speeches by people they don't know in honor of other people they don't know before those people speak for themselves. Every so often, they will be distracted by the swell of a distant cheer coming from a back room, but they won't be able to investigate the sound's origin (a group of tux-clad men who have slipped off to watch the LSU game on TV). For the moment, the queens are simply very pretty furniture.

Eventually, the farmers' speeches are over and the floor is cleared for dancing. Chelsea and the other Visiting Queens have been been released to change out of their mantles and trains. On the portico of the Rice building, the air is hot and thick with mosquitoes when Chelsea emerges, train removed, but only her physical burden lifted. She looks a little tired and a lot wistful. "I guess I'll be 'the girl who got stuck,' now, huh?" she says ruefully, but she actually sounds relieved to have it over.

She hadn't quite pictured her night going this way, but she'll live. And, honestly, it's not really the train incident that has her feeling blue; it's Jace. The truth about being a festival queen is that you must smile through your duties even when things aren't going well elsewhere in your life. It's not as if a satin banner with your name on it offers you any protection from disappointments and heartache. Your crown has no magic properties when you're at work, around the dinner table with your folks, or dealing with a recalcitrant boyfriend.

She holds up the cell phone that has been an omnipresent part of her attire. All morning, all afternoon, all evening she has been calling and texting, trying to pin Jace down. He'd been jovially noncommittal to the bitter end and then had begged off, using the lame excuse that he had to watch the LSU football game. In Cajun country, that wouldn't ordinarily be a terrible excuse, seeing as the purple-and-gold team is near sacred. But Jace doesn't even like football that much, which means it really *is* just an excuse.

She sighs in frustration. "It's all dissolving quickly. It's affected my schoolwork even. But I don't want it to interfere with this, my one-time opportunity. I don't want to let something so minor as [him skipping an event] blow up and take over my emotions." Admitting that the Jace drama is what kept her so quiet in the field at Cattle, she groans. "I would hate to go to a festival and have people see me as quiet or rude, when it's just *him*."

She wonders aloud if she has a future with Jace, and says she knows she is the only one who can answer that question.

"He should treat me better, and I know I deserve him to. But the one thing I am not is a quitter." Yet is it really giving up, she wonders aloud, if you've tried for two years and the guy still ends up disappointing you time and again? I suggest that if she's a queen now, she should at least find a guy who treats her like a princess. "Yeah," she says, one hand on the door. "I'll tell him that."

She laughs faintly and heads back inside to dance alone.

8

Yes, They Can

As I fly into Lafayette over the cypress swamps, the sunlight seems to move in sync with the tiny plane I share with only three other passengers. Like a directional beam on the water below, the glow is reflected back as a radiant silver finger. *Come this way,* it beckons, flashes of light racing up the snake-like curves of the bayous, occasionally setting whole swamp beds on liquid fire all at once, illuminated trees glowing like matchsticks. Cities train the eye upward with skylines; Cajun country leads you back to earth.

This weekend is Yambilee. At sixty-two years old, Yam—as the girls call it—boasts a storied past as one of the state's oldest continuously running festivals and the only one to send its queen every single year to D.C. Mardi Gras ball. It's surprising, then, that in recent years the festival has been dogged by a slur, repeated again and again, and always off record: Yam is "dangerous."

"Dangerous" is a loaded term in many parts of Louisiana, a code word that too often seems to mean "black" or "poor."

Opelousas, where Yam is held, is one of the state's few majority black towns, and a comparatively poor one, with a median income of only $16,000, well below the state average. The truth, however, is that the violent crime rates for murder, rape, robbery, and assault in Opelousas are not only lower than the national average, but lower than most of the towns I have already visited, and about which no one felt I needed a warning.

So what accounts for the whispers about Yam? The root is a story that makes it sound as if white queens are endangered if they ride in the Grand Parade. In one version, when the royal floats (bearing the Yambilee court and the Visiting Queens) made their way down the main drag in 2007, every single crowned head was white, which set off the crowd. First, just words flew: "Where are the black girls?" and "Who made you queen?" And then it was cups and plastic water bottles. No one was physically hurt, and the barrage didn't last long, but the queens were scared. Or so went the story, which got repeated often enough and with so many variations that some directors no longer want their queens to ride in the parade.

But here's the catch: It didn't happen. Brandy was on the float of legend in 2007 and she never had anything thrown at her at all; moreover, she was also there the year before, and it didn't happen then, either. She, too, had heard the rumor— back in 2006, when she was crowned Yambilee Queen, someone told her it had happened the year before that. (She did hear complaints from local people that the queen was always white, but never in any threatening way.) Queens who rode in Yambilee as far back as 2003 all said the same thing: It didn't happen to *them*, either. As far as I could tell, the grain of truth in the rumor—that some hard feelings exist about the whiteness of the event—had been turned around into an attack on the people who felt this way, and ramped up into a myth that only made things worse.

This reflects a bigger issue in the festival pageant world: While all other festival events—parades, carnivals, concerts—are attended in great number by Louisianians of all races, festival pageants nearly uniformly draw white crowds and crown white queens. In a state whose population is nearly one-third black, no more than five or six of its Miss festival queens a year are girls of color, and only once in its half-century run has Queen of Queens ever crowned a black contestant as its winner. Imagine, then, being a person of color living in Opelousas, coming out for decades to watch the big parade that annually fills your hometown's streets. Yes, you'll have witnessed marching bands with high-schoolers of all races, and have seen an increasingly diverse slate of elected officials waving from the backseats of convertibles over the years. But most years when the Visiting Queens' float rolled into view, it was white girl sitting by white girl sitting by white girl. And every single time the Yambilee Royalty float rounded the corner, both its queen and king were white. You could be forgiven for complaining after sixty years. But the world spins in only one direction: forward. Maybe this year will put both painful myth and past reality to bed.

In the Yambilee building, contestants, parents, and visiting queens are getting ready for the weekend. While many festivals separate out their pageants from their festivals by a week or more, Yambilee crowns its queen during the festivities. The carnival midway opened last night, and tomorrow is the Grand Louisiyam Parade, while today's highlights are the Queen's Luncheon, in honor of the outgoing queen, and the crowning of her successor this evening. The entire weekend is rife with humorous rituals, including the decoration of Yamimals: one "odd-shaped" yam left whole and in its "natural color," but decorated so as to resemble a living creature. The luncheon about to begin is no exception, as its centerpiece is a Burlap Sack Parade for the Visiting Queens.

Each queen wears an outfit made of burlap sacks, a staple of agricultural life. The girls mill about, comparing outfits, some happier with their attire than others. Delcambre Shrimp has fringed her sack dress in pale pink marabou feathers that match the jewel version of a cooked shrimp at the center of her crown. Hot Sauce sports an orange pepper-studded minidress so tight and short that she won't easily be able to sit without causing a stir. Gueydan Duck stands out with her duck-call whistle and a huge burlap poncho, emblazoned with a mural of a duck blind, topped with a fringe of feathers (which she admits she did not pluck but instead purchased at Michael's craft store).

Strawberry looks beautiful in a completely tailored dress, dyed deep pink and adorned with appliquéd seeds, but to her annoyance, people keep asking if she's the Watermelon Queen instead. Over and over, less patiently each time, she explains that a watermelon has black seeds and the seeds on her dress are white, which means she's Strawberry.

Chelsea loves this sort of thing—any chance to show off Frog lore in a new way—but she won't be here for hours. She was up at five A.M. today getting ready for the Buddy Walk in Lafayette, a fund-raiser for services provided to Down syndrome children. She goes to the walk every year, but this time she gets to wear her Frog Queen banner and crown, adding extra sparkle to the walkathon. The downside of her participation is that she has to miss out on the Yam events in the meantime.

The organizers tell the burlap-clad girls here to line up for their presentation, and they head for the stage. Miss Acadiana, Yuwa Vosper, steps onto the stage, and her presence is the first hint that this is a year that will defy stereotypes; it makes a difference to have a woman of color at the front as the voice of experience. Yuwa is not dressed in costume, instead wearing a sleek little T-shirt and jeans ensemble that shows off her athletic figure, but she holds up a burlap yam sack and says that she brought it to show solidarity. As emcee, she calls the girls out one by one, commenting on each as they pass.

At the head of the line is Brandy, who has thrown herself into her first duty back on the queen circuit with gusto. Unlike Catfish, who had an aunt tailor, dye, and bedazzle her almost too-perfect outfit, Brandy has made her own ensemble by hand. She has fashioned a fitted thigh-length tunic that crisscrosses over her shoulders in thick cotton-blossom straps and boasts fluffy cotton buttons. Yuwa instructs the audience to check out the back of Brandy's tunic, which is emblazoned with the familiar industry slogan: "The Fabric of Our Lives."

Right behind Brandy is Kristen, her minidress a study in brevity, the effect ramped up with black leather go-go boots that would read vampy on anyone but Kristen, who has also affixed an adorable cow face with an actual bell to her outfit. Yuwa can't think what to call the black-on-white pattern that outlines the strapline and hem of the dress. "Here is the Cattle Queen in . . . what? Cow spots?"

Kristen offers up, "Just call it moo print!"

In a room not short on people with farm backgrounds, that answer is less than persuasive. "Oh, for God's sake," a woman mutters behind me. "It's holstein."

Lauren sits, sackless, watching the parade. With college to finish paying for and graduation looming, she has stopped buying materials to make craft projects every time a festival asks. She makes no apologies for not having the free time or extra cash necessary to pull off the Yam sack ensemble this weekend, and this policy is global: She isn't planning on buying and decorating Wellingtons for Strawberry or building a Fur-themed sled for levee races at Bonfire. With all the demands on her time, some things remain and some things do not. Travel? Yes. Speak passionately on behalf of her festival? Yes. Play Martha Stewart in overalls? No, sir.

For the girls running to be Yambilee Queen, the day's competition has its whimsical moments, even as they pursue the more serious goal of being chosen to represent the festival. Their attire reflects both sides of this equation: playful hats paired with conservative suits. Snug cloches and *Gone With the Wind* bonnets and Sunday-churchgoing affairs gussied up with ribbons or feathers, the hats are a Yambilee tradition that lends a lighthearted Southern elegance to the proceedings while paying tribute to the era more than sixty years past when this festival began.

Blame it on the rumors, or call it a fluke, but one week ago, no one was running for this storied crown at all, a scenario Yam had never before faced. So Brandi Zeringue, the pageant director, found herself calling directors in other parishes and towns, asking them to spread the word, which in turn flew across the Voy boards. As a result, eight girls have now hastily assembled for the competition, none of them new to the boards. In fact, Lauren, Brandy, Kristen, and Chelsea have each previously competed against at least one of these girls before, including Hope, now on her fourth pageant in two months. Hope isn't alone as a former titlist; among them, these eight girls are already in possession of eleven old festival banners, reading Teen Yam, Church Buggy, Mayhaw, Cajun, Forest, Orange, Shrimp, Honey Bee, Cypress Swamp, Swamp Pop, and Meat Pie.

For now, the contestants must wait to see who among them will add a title. The only prize this afternoon is for Best Burlap Sack, and the same judges who will crown tonight's Yam Queen pick a winner: Brandy. It's a silly thing, really, and yet still a nice validation of her return to the circuit, and she radiates satisfaction as the noon event draws to a close.

The Visiting Queens head for a Yambilee board member's home to pass the midday hours before the evening pageant. It is a cloudless fall day, too cold perhaps for the beach, but warm enough for Cattle and Hot Sauce to sit dangling their legs in the water of a pool, while the other girls sun them-selves on the home's back steps, their conversations accompa-nied by the music of a "Cajun Wind Chime," a collection of beer bottles hung like a mobile.

This isn't leisure time for Lauren. At this very moment, a laptop as wide as her waist is perched on her knees, and she peers through dark sunglasses at the screen while rummaging through stacks of papers on sociology and world health with her free hand. Though things are starting to settle down on the home front—she's talking to her dad, and her sister is out of the hospital—she's still a college senior with a thirty-hour-a-week job. There's really no such thing as an afternoon to kill.

As of last week, there's a new wrinkle in Lauren's sched-ule: The terms of her Fur contract have just changed. The damage from Ike has proved crippling to Cameron Parish and, by extension, its festival. The board looked at the hard, windswept reality of their lives—five out of seven of them made homeless by the storm—and has grimly voted to can-cel the festival and its pageant. That doesn't mean Fur can do without a queen; the festival still needs a girl who will cross the state explaining what has happened to them, and promis-ing people that someday Fur will come back. The board wants—it *needs*—Lauren.

When pageant director Ms. Vicki called Lauren and asked her to be queen for a second year, she was shocked. "I was supposed to give up my title in January. I mean it, I was *done*," she tells me. From working at a fund-raiser in Cameron for a girl who'd been injured in a car accident to mucking about in the fields at Strawberry on the opposite end of the state, she has already logged thousands of miles and hundreds of hours for this title. "I was looking forward to free time—wait, what is free time, again?"

She knew if she said yes, she'd still be queen while turning twenty-three, the cut-off age for Miss queens, which would make her just about the Oldest Living Festival Queen, surrounded by supposed peers as young as sixteen. And she knows that not everyone respects a title that is appointed, instead of competed for. But Lauren, like so many festival queens, is a keener, a girl who sees no task she can't meet. Once she sets her jaw to something, the universe may as well bend to her will; if the festival respects her enough to ask, then of course her crazy schedule can be mastered for another semester, and no small thing like potential gossip will dissuade her. She said yes.

In the week since, she has been rewarded with negative posts on the Voy board, some asking why Fur couldn't still have a pageant, even with the festival canceled, and others suggesting that since Lauren had already been festival queen for a year, maybe the title should be given to the parish queen instead. Not one person posting criticized her behavior or representation of the festival, but still they were happy to tarnish her agreement to continue her reign, some invoking the dreaded slur Crown Chaser—though in this case, the crown had clearly chased her.

"At first my feelings were really hurt," she tells me. "I had worked so hard for Fur, and then this?" So here she sits, suddenly facing fourteen more months of duties instead of two, schoolwork preventing her from just relaxing, and still subject to criticism by strangers. But she really isn't complaining that much. "I can deal," she says, and then laughs. "Unless I don't finish my homework."

As the hour of the pageant approaches, the jeans are sloughed off, the ponytails shaken out, the sneakers traded for heels. The girls shimmy into silky evening gowns, affix glittering earrings, don makeup that can stand up to spotlights, and emerge from hotel rooms as thoroughly transformed as Clark Kent, if not quite as rapidly.

Chelsea is one of the first to arrive at the Yambilee building, and she has made up for missing the Burlap Parade by carrying the Frog theme into her attire, which is thoroughly green from gown to mantle. For a girl who worked an eight-hour shift to close the store last night and then rose before dawn for a walkathon, Chelsea looks fresh and energetic. She loves the pageantry of being a festival queen, and now that she's had a little experience maneuvering in her regalia, she's less nervous about tonight. The only hard part for a shy girl is stepping into an event like this one after all the other girls have already been here all day, their groove established without her. But Kristen, in black-and-white lace, bounds over to say hello and take a picture with Chelsea, which takes the edge off and draws her into the mix. Soon they are headed off to the Yambilee version of a greenroom, which I call the Coop.

The buildings of the festival world, premised on agricultural and industrial roots, rarely match the loveliness of the queen's attire, and Yambilee's is no exception. The auditorium is composed of your basic concrete flooring and cinder-block walls, and that's the *pretty* part. The gathering area for the visiting queens looks a bit like a cross between a henhouse and a meth lab. The eight-by-ten space has one wall entirely covered in chicken wire, affixed to wooden slats. Under fluorescent lights, the girls' gowns all take on a gray-green glow, the hems trailing onto dusty concrete. The closest thing to decoration is the unframed full-length mirror screwed into place on a scarred plywood wall. In a movie, this room is where a serial killer would bring his victims, or perhaps the place where one would hide out from zombies only to realize how thin plywood walls are. But these are festival queens, not princesses, and they neither notice nor care. Despite arriving late, Chelsea is now in the thick of things, listening to Kristen tell a story, while Brandy checks messages on her cell phone, and Lauren leans against the wall, her fur banner providing a soft cushion against the rough wood.

Awaiting their audience, they seem a natural unit, as comfortable as choir members shooting the breeze in the balcony of a church before services begin. Yet because of the fluid nature of the festival season, these specific emissaries have never all been together at once; at each event there is a slight re-calibration of the dynamic, allowing for recent friends lost and new friendships developed. Moreover, it is a social network crowded with history, and more than one of these queens has previously lost a much-desired crown to another girl in the Coop.

It was two years ago that Brandy and Lauren vied for Yambilee Queen in this very building. Back then, they were rivals who knew each other only as past Shrimp and Andouille Queens. On the day of the pageant, Lauren pulled into the parking lot just before Brandy and her mom. When Brandy saw Lauren get out of her car, she turned to her mom and said, "I want to leave right now." Having only worn a local crown, Brandy felt intimidated by a girl who had two wins, including a state title, but her mom pressed her to go inside and just have fun. Brandy was wearing a blue hat-and-suit ensemble for the judges' interview, and she hadn't doubted the appropriateness of her outfit until the contestants were gathered to choose Miss Congeniality. She heard a voice behind her say, "Oh, don't worry about her. She looks like a big blueberry." When she turned around, the subject had changed, but the nearest person in her line of sight was Lauren. Brandy went red and headed for the car, thinking she shouldn't have come in the first place, but her mom reined her in, pointing out that if she quit, the gossipers would win.

As luck would have it, the title came down to Brandy and Lauren. Lauren was named runner-up and felt devastated, thinking, *I won the first two—this isn't how it goes.* Brandy, still burning from the insult even in her triumph, turned to Lauren and whispered, "I guess they like blueberries." As Brandy was whisked away for photos, Lauren stood there baffled. *Blueberries?*

When Brandy told her old director what had happened, the story spread and soon the stiletto was on the other foot, with people talking about what a bitchy thing Lauren had said. Except that Lauren denied saying it, and her friends backed her up. She took the bull by the horns and called Brandy to say so, and Brandy began to regret talking about it, as she really had never seen the speaker. Emotionally, it was a bad deal for both of them, and though they officially cleared the air at the time, there was no great affection between them. But this year, when Lauren sided with Brandy at the Cotton pageant and then they spent more time together at the festival as mutual friends of the outgoing queen, they began to really click. Now the blueberry incident is a ruefully funny anecdote that they tell together. In the Coop tonight, they are clearly a team.

The girls are warned that it's almost time for their entries, which means time to don their mantles. This is a two-person task for most of them, seeing as they must lift the enormous fans over their heads, and then cinch them into place with various snaps and straps. The outgoing queen, Lindsey Cooper, doesn't even try to crowd into the Coop, but dons her Yam wings out in the main room by the buffet tables, with a friend tugging and pulling at the laces with the fervor of a Victorian corset maker.

At a glance, one might think Lindsey had wandered into

the festival world by accident, so clearly does she look the part of Miss USA: tall, blond, statuesque, the perfect glamazon. But being a bombshell doesn't inherently make you insubstantial. Lindsey is a paralegal with a serious passion for her festival, ever ready with a hellfire-and-brimstone lecture on the topic. "Yambilee used to be integral to the Yam industry, but that hasn't been as true in recent years, so I was determined to restore our place. I attended Yam commission meetings, agricultural board meetings, and statewide industry events." She wants a successor who will do all of that, even if it means not making it to all the fairs and festivals. "It's not about getting to Our Lady of the Charm Bracelet. It's about honoring your industry and making a difference. When you represent a commodity, you have to step up."

Small wonder that her director, Ms. Brandi, says a little nervously, "The girls have *big* shoes to follow."

Fortunately, one of the judges is an expert in this regard. Renee Berger is back at the Yambilee pageant after thirty years away. When she won the crown herself three decades ago, she went from being a quiet eighteen-year-old girl to a commanding presence who snagged 1st runner-up at Queen of Queens and then took over the title when the winner stepped down early. In the decades since, she has lived all over the country and worked in the hotel industry, rising to the position of vice president in her most recent job. When asked what part, if any, Yambilee Queen played in her eventual career trajectory, she is emphatic: "It made me everything I am. It taught me responsibility to community. It taught me confidence. And that the true meaning of competition is to find a passion." That's what she wants to see tonight: passion, poise, and goals.

In a moment that sums up the staying power of festivals, an elderly man approaches Renee as we speak. She doesn't recognize him, but it is clear that he remembers her fondly, as he takes her hand in both of his, the sleeves of his suit receding nearly to his elbows, exposing frail forearms. She leans in to hear him speak in a rasping whisper. "I was here the night you were crowned, and I still remember it!" he tells her. For him, seeing her here after all this time is equal parts celebrity sighting and homecoming weekend, her success proof positive that they picked the right girl.

Now it's her turn to choose wisely as the pageant begins and we all take our places: Renee at the judges' table, the girls backstage, and me at a table with Chelsea's mom, and Kristen's mom and grandmother. The silver-haired emcee, an amalgam of carnival barker and Bob Barker, croons, "Behind this curtain, beautiful young ladies wait."

When we finally meet the contestants, my tablemates and I start playing the guess-the-winner game. Will it be #1, the Miss Louisiana Cajun who wants to be a nurse but currently works both on a hog farm and at Winn-Dixie? Or #2, the former Miss Slidell who was recently a Honeybee Queen? How will the judges distinguish between #3 and #4, one working in a law office and the other for the attorney general's office? Will there be a hometown edge for the past Teen Yambilee Queen, whose senior-high résumé is plump with cheerleading, tumbling, mock trial, class vice presidency, and

National Honor Society? Will contestant #6's big aims—a Ph.D. in psychology—be overshadowed by her tiny arms, the kind of skin-on-bone limbs that have some observers whispering? As a former Forest Festival and Swamp Pop Queen, contestant #7 packs dual crowns and poise to match, but then so does Hope as contestant #8, so familiar a face now that she earns the biggest cheers from the Visiting Queens, and a cry of "That's my baby!" from her mother, sitting near the front.

While representatives from the local accounting firm hired by Yambilee sit at their own table, crunching the numbers provided by the judges, Queen Moms compare notes. Chelsea's mom, Vicki, thinks #1 or #7, but Kristen's mom, Lisa, disagrees, pegging #2 or #5. In both cases, they're pitting back-story (hog farmer, senior class all-star) against polish (queens with two or three titles under their belts). From where she sits, Brandy doesn't see the choice in those terms; having been a Yambilee Queen, she thinks the judges are looking for state title confidence. Her money is on two of the multi-titled girls, #2 and #7, with #4, the more glamorous of the two legal eagles, thrown into the mix. And she's right: The judges pick exactly those girls (sending poor Hope to her fourth loss in a row).

Among the three finalists, their qualifications alone do not make any one stand out (among them, they represent six past festival titles), and their onstage interviews are not definitive, all three answering a question about aid to Yam farmers with pleasant but slightly wobbly replies. The biggest impression made at this point is inadvertent—when they call #7, she is still in the bathroom and so does not appear. And does not appear. And does not appear. When she finally hurries in, she is a little out of breath and red-cheeked, which softens her quite a bit, from an almost too-perfect beauty earlier in the evening to a much more human look, a girl with a self-deprecating laugh and good spirit in the face of a somewhat embarrassing moment. This may well have done the trick: Meghin Frazier, nineteen years old, is the Yambilee Queen.

As the pageant breaks up, the first people to show up at the judges' table are Hope and her mother. One can only imagine what they are asking, what they are feeling. And how little a judge can say, except that which been said to a thousand girls before her: *It just wasn't your night.*

Sunday comes on hot. Parade participants fill the marshaling area along the two-lane road running in front of Ray's & Billy's Boudin, a popular market where women stir roiling kettles of pork skin behind the counter. Business is brisk as folks dart in for bottles of water and pop, and the latest batch of cracklins served up in brown bags, the pale paper translucent with redolent drippings.

At the front of the parade ranks is Gueyland LeDay, at eleven years old the youngest parade marshal in Yambilee history, and also African-American—an inspired choice to lead the throng. A zydeco accordionist who started playing at age three, he's been on the *Ellen* show and HBO and even won an Oscar Mayer commercial contest, all while still going to school right here in his hometown. Though perhaps the most famous, he's not the only young performer getting ready to face the crowds. Down the street, the little girls of PJ's Dance Art School are practicing their moves in white T-shirts emblazoned with their mission: *Praise Dancers for God*.

The tiny dancers look more comfortable at this moment than the Visiting Queens, gathering roadside by their float, with neither cloud nor cypress to soften the sun's insistent glare. Their ride is a hay wagon lined with yam crates and burlap sacks, the only seats being the pair of back-to-back wooden benches smack in the middle. Not all of the queens present the day before have returned. Chelsea, who had been warned that the parade would not be a pleasant experience, didn't bother trying to get out of work at Buckle. And Brandy, having done back-to-back Yambilee parades in 2006 and 2007, is at work, too. But the smaller numbers is a good thing: This wagon is suited for maybe a dozen queens at best, and those in attendance fit just about right, as long as they sit cheek to cheek and back to back.

Lauren sits at the head of the float, despite how she actually feels about this task. "Honestly, riding in a parade is one of my least favorite things to do. You're always going to have people yelling at you and people telling you how to wave—as if all queens should wave like they are the queen of England! But I do it because it comes with the job. And it's the times you see that one little girl's face light up when you pass and wave to her that makes the task much more enjoyable!"

She is joined by Queen Sugar, a brassy blonde with a smoker's voice who shames me for carrying a diet soda containing a sugar substitute. Yuwa climbs aboard and sits dead center, so that spectators cannot miss the strong, beautiful black woman in this year's contingent. Strawberry, Hot Sauce, Celtic Nations, Spice, and St. Charles surround her. On the opposite side of the float sits Crawfish, and even though she brought the wrong outfit for such a hot day—expecting cold, she packed a turtleneck and a belted jumper—she says she loves every moment of her reign. She grew up in Breaux Bridge and, at age five, announced that she would be Crawfish Queen someday, then waited patiently the dozen years until she was old enough to run, and did in fact win it on her first try. She is adamant that this crown will be her last. "In my town, once you've been Crawfish, you've lived the dream."

Next to Crawfish, Kristen brings up the rear. She's brought one bag of candy, but when she discovers that Yam hasn't provided anything else for the Visiting Queens to throw, she gets a little nervous. "This isn't gonna last a whole parade!" On only her third parade, she already understands that empty hands are *not* a welcome sight to spectators.

The Visiting Queen float looks humble comparatively because all the glitter went to the biggest float in the parade. The new Yam royalty are perched high on a multilevel trailer, the Queen in gown and mantle sitting beside a man who is making history today. Lloyd Price is the first-ever African-American Yambilee King. An R&B musician known for his songs "Personality," "Stagger Lee," and "Lawdy, Miss Clawdy," Price is also a yam champion, owner of Lawdy, Miss Clawdy Foods, a line of yam-based goods so popular that his was the first black-owned company with a Wal-Mart contract. Resplendent in his tux jacket, he's the first person of color to sit atop this float in sixty years, and he radiates happy satisfaction. (Though he doesn't know it, in a year's time, a girl from Opelousas will climb up onto this perch and grace the float as the first-ever African-American Yambilee Queen.)

The pickup truck pulling the Visiting Queen float lurches into motion, and the royals roll toward the crowds. Block by block, they pass families in lawn chairs, tailgate parties in parking lots, and people of all races together and apart. Some of the spectators tease the girls—"Nothing? Ya got nothing?"—and the girls play along, pretending to throw invisible beads or picking up crates and sacks as if they might heave them. But the queens face no hostility today, no anger, no danger. The rudest comments that float through the air pertain entirely to the lack of goodies flying back.

There is ample goodwill in Opelousas at this moment, everyone caught in the spell of a brilliant afternoon and the high spirits of a parade. But there is an added burst of pleasure when the royal float turns the final corner downtown and the parade announcer proudly proclaims the historic nature of this year's royalty. The new queen beams at her king as he rises to acknowledge the moment, flashing an electric smile. The crowd lets loose with foot-stomping, whistling joy, a music that follows Their Majesties 'round the bend.

9

Under the Pig Top

You cannot be a festival queen and a priss at the same time. It is simply not possible to keep your nose in the air while a squealing pig charges toward your legs. A few dozen visiting queens will find that out firsthand this warm November afternoon, as part of the Swine Festival in Basile, where a greasy pig chase awaits them.

The fact that the Swine Festival still features actual swine keeps the event close in spirit to its earliest predecessors. According to Julie Avery's *Agricultural Fairs in America,* the first such fair on our continent was held in October 1810 in the Berkshires in Massachusetts. The entire draw of that first event was this: two sheep tied to a tree in a village square, with farmer Elkanah Watson next to them declaiming their virtues. As he later wrote, "Many farmers and even women were excited by curiosity to attend this first novel and humble exhibition. It was by this lucky accident, I reasoned thus, if two animals are capable of exciting so much attention, what would be the effect on a larger scale?" For Watson, "larger scale" meant

more livestock: a team of sixty-nine oxen drawing a plow at
the direction of the oldest man in the county. Nearly two hundred years later, the Swine Festival organizers have inverted
Watson's formula, rightly surmising that one animal and many
young women will be a bigger draw than many animals and
one old man.

From the various parishes they represent, the would-be
hog-followers begin to arrive five or six hours before they will
be summoned onto the field. Today's uniform is crowns, banners over T-shirts or polos, blue jeans, and sturdy sneakers—
hardly a flip-flop or cute slip-on in sight, as these girls know
what they're getting themselves into. They line up at the front
gate, where five dollars merits them a proof-of-entry wristband in one of several after-dinner-mint shades. Across a patch
of grass rutted with tire tracks, they head for what I'll call the
Pig Top, a hulking barn with a peaked tin roof supported by
sturdy posts but no walls. At one point, this structure was the
open-air trade market for feeder pigs, and it was here that the
Louisiana swine industry association was launched. The dry
land around the Pig Top is flat, so the barn is both anchor and
high point, a metal circus tent. The few food vendors are tucked
in close, as are the handful of worn-looking carnival rides on
the building's back side, which makes this by far the most com-
pact festival I've seen: It could fit snugly inside the gridiron of
a football field.

The crowds at this point number in the hundreds, not
thousands. The small size of Swine is one of its virtues; the
town of Basile is home to only sixteen hundred people, so at-

tracting modest crowds to its festival keeps the event from
losing its identity as a local community celebration. There is a
distinctly relaxed, down-home feeling under the Pig Top, as if
it were a very well-attended family reunion, which in some
ways it is.

Cindy Fontenot Smith, the Swine Festival Association
secretary, grew up here and has attended Swine for her entire
life. Even though she now farms crawfish, rice, and soybeans
up Route 190 in the even tinier town of Swords, Swine remains a core part of her life: a labor of love, a tradition so important to her family that not only is she working Swine this
year, but so are her three sisters, who together compose more
than half the board. This makes them a busy quartet this
weekend. From the pageant to the parade to the pork cook-
off, there's a Fontenot in charge at every turn. There's a sister
at the gate right now, handing over pastel wristbands to late-
arriving queens, who must hurry into the barn for the first of
their duties.

Brandy is here with her mom, and they're both enjoying
having the same day free of work; her mom works all week as
a home babysitter, and Brandy often works nights and weekends, so time together is rare and precious. Chelsea has a crew
in tow: The Tadpole, Deb, Junior, Teen, and Ms. Frog Queens
have also come, all but Ms. in matching T-shirts, which makes
it hard to miss the Frog presence. Kristen is doing her festival
duties elsewhere—she's attending the Cut Off Hurricane
Queen pageant (Cut Off being the town, Hurricane being
just what it sounds like). Lauren is also missing, hard at work

at the boutique, which is dressing several competitors for tonight's Miss Louisiana USA pageant.

Swine requires more of the Visiting Queens than just the pig chase: Hours before they take to the field for the running of the swine, the queens must take part in the boudin-eating contest. One of the most iconic foods of Cajun country, boudin is a chubby sleeve of sausage casing stuffed with a moist (if slightly unsettling) blend of rice, pork liver, and pork heart. If your boudin is dark, it probably also contains pig blood, which makes it more intense. At the Swine Festival, there are boudin-eating contests throughout the day, including one just for the Visiting Queens, who must speedily consume a boudin log the size of a fat baby doll arm. One queen told me you don't really eat it, you "stuff it"—just shove the whole thing in your mouth and chew it enough to go down.

The girls gather around a long wooden banquet table set beneath the Pig Top, as the emcee encourages festivalgoers to come watch the queens make hogs of themselves. This is the subliminal advertising of the fair world: The audience thinks they're watching a goofy ritual, but they are also absorbing reminders of upcoming festivals, the names of which are stitched onto banners or emblazoned on T-shirts. Brandy, in her sky-blue Cotton Festival shirt, takes up a spot at one corner of the table just down from Chelsea, whose pink top features Monsieur Jacques, the Frog icon. Miss Queens like them are joined by queens in other age divisions, some as young as thirteen and the oldest at fifty-two. For this least dainty of tasks before them, they are each given a modest white paper napkin and then handed logs of meat and rice.

On "Go!" the eating begins, with the crowd whooping it up behind the contestants. Some girls are breaking apart the boudin into bite-size pieces, while others keep it whole and start from one end, as you would with beef jerky. Chelsea and Brandy both use a pincher approach: They hold their sausages with two hands, thumbs and forefingers forming tiny vises, remaining fingers extended, as if they are holding tea sandwiches or demitasse cups instead of swine organs. Chelsea is not a big eater in general, so she's not racing along here, and though Brandy likes boudin, the piece is simply bigger than she's willing to stuff. This makes them no match for eaters who do just shove the whole damn thing into their mouths, and it is only a few seconds before two cries of victory go up nearly simultaneously. Ms. Frog, a former Queen of Queens who knows her way around festival sports, throws her arms in the air at one end of the table, just as Cajun Food does the same thing at the opposite end. The judges immediately decree a tie, and no one calls for an instant replay or a stuff-off, because festival duties are really less about the winning than the doing. (Ms. Frog admits, though, that she can't help herself, and laughs, "I'm competitive. If I have to kick and elbow, I will.")

As the girls wipe their mouths and now-greasy fingers, the DJ cues up the music. The radio hit "Cupid Shuffle" comes on, and girls fall into rows as automatically as if programmed by a hypnotist. The lyrics are barely more than instructions—"To the left, to the left, to the left, to the left, to the right, to the right, to the right, to the right"—but damn if it isn't catchy, linking a hooky tune to easy steps, repeated endlessly until you can do them without thinking. Created by a Louisiana musician whose name it bears, "Cupid Shuffle" may be the first zydeco hip-hop country line dance ever, a God-bless-America multi-culti mash-up.

The girls applaud as the song dies down, and they clear the floor when the headliner is announced: Geno Delafose & French Rockin' Boogie, a zydeco combo composed of vocals, scrub board (an instrument worn like a metal vest), accordion, and guitar. The band fills the barn with swirling, upbeat music, which draws two-stepping couples onto the floor, the average age of dancer shooting up a few decades in the changeover.

Beyond the cool shade of the Pig Top, it's easy to spot the Swine royalty in their white T-shirts emblazoned with hogs. As befitting the host festival, they have the most royalty here: not only a Deb, Teen, Miss, and Ms., but a Jr. Teen, Petite Miss, and, smallest of all, Queen Petunia, a toddler still young enough to be sucking her thumb for all the photos and begging to be carried everywhere. Just as Chelsea is the Frog of Frogs in Rayne, the Top Hog here is the wearer of the Miss Queen crown: a towering diadem with a Porky Pig–like centerpiece crafted of pink jewels (swinestones, if you will).

To talk to Swine, you are first likely to have to get through her father, who darts constantly into the scene to introduce himself or take pictures, his camera wet with sweat. He's an arm-grabber, a person-steerer, leading you to pay attention to what he is talking about, keeping you in place while he speaks. Brandy is polite when he gloms on to her as she bonds with the Swine Queen over both being twenty-two in a system full of younger girls, but when he steps away for a moment, she tries to get a handle on him. "Wow—he takes a lot of pictures," she says. Swine smiles as if to say, *He is what he is.*

Swine takes everything in stride, at least in public. She comes from the glitz pageant circuit, where she's won multiple titles, and she knows that some people resent it when glitz girls nab festival crowns. (Because glitz competitions are all about a girl's looks and, unlike in a festival, her win serves no larger purpose, there is little traffic between the two worlds.) But Swine doesn't care about such separations: She just likes to compete and last year held a civic title, Miss Church Point. During that reign, she attended Swine and met the girl who would become her predecessor. "The queen giving up her title was so friendly and spontaneous, and Swine was so fun." She liked the spirit of the event immediately and threw herself into the day, nabbing her first victory in Basile: "I caught the pig."

When she returned this year to compete for the crown, she says, "I put my all into it. I studied till I was blue in the face, and it showed." Though she faced backlash even before the pageant was over, competing as she was against a proven festival queen, she wasn't surprised to win. Her victory occasioned pages of commentary on the Voy boards, with detractors lobbing bombs like the claim that she's secretly a stripper.

Sitting on a playground swing next to the midway, long legs dragging in the grass, the new Swine Queen seems unfazed. Tossing her shoulder-length hair, she adopts a look that is part pout, part smirk. "When I saw it, I thought the Voy stuff was funny. And, honestly, I got my little moment of fame. What can I say?"

She's got more important things to consider than rumors. Having been Swine Queen for all of one week, she's already thinking of her future competition at Queen of Queens and says, "I'm very excited and I'm ready for it." Though the competition is still three months away, she has a look in her eye like the look a pitcher gives before hurling a fastball. "I just got my crown, but I promise you, I'm *ready*."

As she heads back into the Pig Top for a photo op, the midway is full of Visiting Queens, including the oldest contestant from the boudin contest. Plump, with friendly eyes disappearing into wrinkles, fifty-two-year-old Janice Guillroy holds the title of Evangeline Parish She's My Grandma Queen. I ask how she came to hold this title and she says her daughter talked her into it. As if on cue, daughter Kayla appears, with Janice's granddaughter on her hip. Kayla explains that they're a festival-loving family. She's the current Ms. Queen, two age categories down from her mom in the same royal court, and her toddler has already been Baby Miss Swine. And the Guillroys are hardly alone in this. Some family names seem inextricably woven into local festival traditions. The Bergeron and Landry families have both boasted mother-daughter-granddaughter trios all serving as festival queens in the same year. And then there's the Johnson family: Mom was an Orange Queen and Dad was King Cotton Boll; their twin girls split the legacy, one as Queen Cotton and the other Orange Queen. But perhaps the ultimate royals are the Arceneaux family: The parents met as King and Queen Strawberry, fell in love and married, and raised two daughters who both went on to become Strawberry Queen, the elder crowning the younger as her successor. In families like these, festivals are written into the DNA.

The sun is just barely sloping downward as the girls are called to a pig field large enough for a regulation football game. Hemmed in by a chain-link fence, the grass is the color of late summer in the country, not the vivid green of a manicured lawn, but more sun-baked, with earth showing through—the kind of field where a queen stampede will kick up serious clods. Brandy and her mom head the other way, not because Brandy is afraid to touch a swine (she's done the pig chase before) but because time is precious for both. "We're going to go shopping together while we can because my mom is tied to the house the rest of the week." Plus, she wouldn't mind getting out of there because neither of them is having a good day on the diet front. Brandy has kept her weight off so far, but days like this are a test. They leave before they can do any more damage.

Chelsea stays. Tomorrow it's back to work at Buckle, where some of her coworkers have been carping about how many weekend days she has already taken off. She doesn't think of Saturdays like this as days off: For her it's still a workday.

Her work is representing Frog, and productivity means eating boudin and chasing a pig, so she's halfway there. She lines up with Rice and Hot Sauce and a dozen or so others, as a young farmhand slathers a short black pig with Vaseline. Spectators gather along the fence that outlines the field, ready for a good laugh.

The pig chase represents what makes festivals so great: the way humor and history can intersect, grand traditions that don't put on airs. It's a chance to feast on joy, to ditch the cynical side of modern life and embrace old-fashioned play. You can see it at the Orange Festival, when the queens line up facing the audience to stuff their mouths full with up to two dozen kumquats, until their cheeks bulge impossibly. And this is true beyond Louisiana: In Ontario, Canada, the Binder Twine Festival puts girls through a variety of odd paces, from hog-calling to wig-braiding to nail-pounding.

Earlier this year, when I attended the Rhododendron Festival (known as Rhody) in Port Townsend, Washington, I witnessed the traditional moment during the parade when a fishmonger knelt before the royal court and presented a large freshly gutted king salmon to the horrified Rhody Queen, a vegetarian who reached out and gingerly accepted her scaly trophy, then sat with it on her lap for the next hour as the parade wrapped up, hoping it wouldn't leak all over her banner.

But of all the festivals I attended, the Vinton County Wild

Turkey Festival in Ohio had the most enigmatic schedule: "Queen Contestants introduced at 6:30; Turkey Drop at 7." *Drop* here is both a verb *and* a noun—which is to say that the center of the event is turkey poop. This is how it works: Fairgoers buy one of a hundred raffle tickets, corresponding to a large grid containing the same number of squares. At the specified time, a wild turkey is turned loose on the grid, free to wander about as he sees fit until the spirit moves him to drop (verb) a drop (noun) onto one of the numbered squares, thus ending the Drop (another noun, if you're counting), and making a winner of the person holding the similarly numbered raffle ticket. Whatever genius of rural entertainment programming dreamed this up, I applaud him.

The swine at the center of things this waning afternoon in Basile doesn't get off quite as easily as that turkey. Once his bristly black fur has been smeared good and thick with Vaseline, he is released from the grip of his teenage holder to face down twenty humans intent on tackling him. The girls let out cheers and war cries as they run toward him, a veritable mob thundering his way, and he does the smart thing: He turns around and runs toward his pen. But the teen handler knows nobody came here to watch a pig outsmart queens, so the boy plays goalie, his boot the stick smacking away a warm bristled puck. Grunting, the pig decides to face his fate, and charges directly toward the queens. For all their bravado, many of the queens now slow down their run, looks of horror creasing their pretty faces. Chelsea drops back, way back, and she isn't alone. A half dozen other girls keep running up front, even while leaning backward away from the pig, a physics trick that makes it look like they are being dragged along reluctantly by their feet.

Only the serious hog-chasers never slow, following the leather bullet as it shoots right by them, then veers off. Its pursuers look like a school of fish, changing direction together in one fluid motion. The Rice Queen pulls ahead until she almost has the pig, her white fingers raking black fur, but it wriggles onward. They run now with desire, arms out, and the pig is slowing, his heavy breathing audible across the grass. Several queens at once conceive of diving to catch him, and down they go, hands grasping for hog and finding only grass, until a thirteen-year-old Junior Queen with the apple-pie name of Betsy Smith hurls herself onto the terrified beast and pins him down. Sweating heavily and breathing hard, she is grinning so broadly that the sunlight glints off her braces. "I should kiss it!" This line, convincingly delivered, merits a chorus of "Eww!" and "Gross!" The other queens physically turn away before she can follow through.

Chelsea feels no shame about her poor hog-catching skills. "I had no intention of catching that greasy ball of stuff! I had a plan: Start off quickly and then fade back, and all the Frog Queens were pretty much thinking the same thing." So why not just skip the field activities entirely? "Because being out here is my job. At the end of the day, every festival queen has to ask herself: Do you sit at home and let your crown get full

of dust, or do you put on your crown and let it get full of festival dirt?"

Chelsea heads for her car. Her big plan for this Saturday
night is to work on a seven-page English paper about the
style of a particular author. It's not due till Monday and she'd
rather go out than work on it, but once again, Jace is unavail-
able. She is getting to a point with Jace that something has to
give. She doesn't like thinking that he takes her for granted so
thoroughly; she likes even less that her acceptance of this
treatment allows for it. A girl who overcame so much to win
Frog ought to have the strength to show a bad boyfriend the
door—but she hasn't yet. She groans just thinking about it.
"Boys . . ."

At the gate, Chelsea walks right by another young woman
who apparently feels the same way, a teenage girl who is be-
rating her boyfriend for spending good money to win a scary
clown mirror when he knows she *hates* clowns. He stares
balefully at his prize, just a moment ago a source of pleasure
and now revealed as tawdry junk. His girlfriend brandishes a
radioactively green slushie, punctuating the end of every exclamation with a jab that threatens to spill the nuclear contents. The couple is still arguing as Chelsea drives away.

Shadows lengthen across the gravel drive, and the tin roof
glows amber in the late light as a dozen or so Harleys roar into
the fairgrounds, the riders all suited up in leather and denim and
bandannas. Hells Angels come to mind but not for long: Once
off their hogs, the entire group politely approaches the gate to
apologize for parking without having yet paid admission. As

docile as schoolchildren or British tourists, they line up, pay five bucks each, and don wristbands, the sweet robin's-egg blue paper adding a cheery note amid all the crossbones and metal studs. One biker says he's ready to dance, and another chimes in he's been dying for a hot dog. Like everyone else, they're just here to have a good time.

10

Her Chariot Awaits

Chelsea is looking at her cell phone. Ms. Cheryl is looking at the calendar. And Pete the frog—well, he's looking at the inside of a bucket and trying to remember life on the outside. It's Frog Festival weekend at last, and everyone has something to be nervous about.

The importance of this weekend to Chelsea can't be overstated. She has spent years imagining what it would be like to reign over this festival as queen, and suddenly it's zero hour for the dream to come true. If she could, she would make time elastic, stretching every moment out beyond the laws of physics, but she knows this weekend will spin onward without slowing, and that all she can do is take it all in, trying to feel every bit of each second intensely before it passes. She also knows that the only way to do that is to leave no room for Jace, not in her weekend, not in her mind, and especially not on her phone. This is not the time to let him play with her emotions, to let his devil-may-care approach to their relationship make her feel unappreciated or second-rate. Not *this* weekend. So she does the unthinkable: She blocks calls from her own boyfriend.

Ms. Cheryl's concerns aren't so easily addressed. Having moved Frog all the way from early September to mid-November—shooting right by eight or nine warmer weeks in between—she has guaranteed that the festival will face no hurricane interruptions or tropical downpours, but risks abound nonetheless: The festival is facing a potential drop-off in attendance due to the unseasonably chilly breeze that plunges the temperatures into the fifties this Friday afternoon, making this the coldest Frog ever. (The temperatures for Frog have reached double that before.) But that's far less worrisome to her than the date change. "It's always been Labor Day weekend or the week after," she says. "People plan their vacations around it. I've done what I can to get the word out, but will people remember that it's this weekend without a holiday to remind them?" If they do forget Frog, the town will feel it: The festival is the primary source of funds for the Chamber of Commerce. Even with a crew of volunteers she describes as amazing, Ms. Cheryl feels the burden. Frog needs thirty thousand or forty thousand people or it's going to hurt.

Poor green Pete, meanwhile, ensconced in his new bucket home, has even less control over his fate. Four girls are competing tomorrow morning to become Frog Derby Queen (the same title that led Chelsea into the festival world). Each contestant has a frog because you can't have a Derby without racing *something*. Maddie Guidry, the contestant who is Pete's keeper, feeds him, exercises him, and croons his name, which makes her a decent warden, all things considered; of course, Pete used to hop through the ponds of Rayne unencumbered and now calls a bucket home, so he might disagree. His future isn't promising: Once he does get free of this pail, Maddie's going to prod him with a stick to make him hop across a cement floor. Worse yet, she's going to dress him up in a costume first. Is this how the town shows love for its icon?

Certainly, in Rayne, frog adoration is clear. Downtown, frog murals catch the eye at every turn, from enormous panoramas taking up entire building walls to wee illustrations the size of a page of notebook paper. Here's a frog version of Thomas Jefferson and there's a frog that changes color when it rains; here's a bullfrog the size of a VW and there's a frog napping in a hammock. It's all frog all the time.

That's because the tiny town lying flat on the Cajun prairie pretty much owes its continued existence to fat frogs. The outgrowth of a railroad stop built in the 1880s, Rayne's first real industry was the packaging and export of local frog legs, the brainchild of French brothers who settled here and noticed that the local "ouaouarons" (the Cajun word for frogs) were awfully meaty. The small settlement's delicacy was soon served all over the globe, from Sardi's in New York to restaurants in Paris, one of which billed Rayne as "The Frog Capital of the World"—a title that stuck. Frogs, as plentiful as they were plump, were so entwined with Rayne's identity that in 1970, when NASA wanted frogs for experiments in space, this was the logical town to turn to. The Chamber of

Commerce Web site still fondly notes that the town's frogs have "boldly gone where no frog had gone before."

If the town is lucky, this love will secure its future. A private-public alliance has been formed between a developer and the city of Rayne to build Frogland USA, a water-theme-park complex, complete with a concert venue, hotels, tennis courts, shops, and restaurants. The price tag isn't cheap— $40 million, by one estimate, with $10 million in tax incentives from the city—but the preliminary plan suggests that the park would generate $2 million a year in local revenue and create seventeen hundred new jobs.

Not all local businesses are crazy about this news. Blake Alleman, one of the siblings who run Gabe's, a family-owned fast-food restaurant deservedly famous for its deep-fried frog legs and crispy chicken, thinks the mom-and-pop shops will lose staff to the proposed complex out on the highway. He waves his hand at the kids working the counter behind him. "If you were a teenage boy, where'd you rather work, where you can see girls in bikinis or in a hot kitchen?" Some folks think he's got nothing to worry about. Just up from Gabe's at the Frog City truck stop, I meet a wizened driver who snaps, "The damn thing costs so much it won't never be built."

That attitude ignores Rayne's history of reinvention. After the frog industry left, followed by the Oil Bust, the town didn't fold up and wither. It made the most of its small attractions— such as the fifty frog murals and the Ripley's Believe It or Not cemetery—to lure busloads of senior tourists. Frogland isn't even the first time that Rayne has looked at an empty field and seen a gold mine. Earlier this decade, the town turned the land around the civic center into an RV park. "At the time, some people couldn't see what an RV park could mean for a community," says Ms. Cheryl, but they sure can now: Roughly three out of four weekends from September to May (the months cool enough for such events) the festival grounds are home to rallies with as many as seven hundred RVs at a time, bringing guests who eat in the town's restaurants, shop in the stores, get their hair done, and even take their pets to Rayne's vet. The effect on the town is both economic and spiritual. "The RV park has been phenomenal—these people become a part of our community."

Right now the fields next to the Civic Center are occupied not with RVs but with the Mitchell Brothers carnival midway, which spreads out beyond the open-sided Frog Pavilion. There are dozens of food booths, rows of rides, and grassy aisles lined with games you can play to win things you don't need. But with the gates not yet open and the carnival crew members not yet at their stations, the midway feels eerily empty. A towering two-story booth rises up from the grass, its first level crowned with a wraparound metal awning, topped by an upper deck composed of an illuminated billboard reading CHICKEN ON A STICK, its slogan accompanied by a photo of skewered tenders larger than the average LSU linebacker. Atop the second story, a dozen red-and-black flags extend the height of the booth even further. As the wind picks up, the flags snap back and forth, fluttering with such intensity that it appears the booth is in motion, a steamer bearing meats into a gaudy harbor. Potted plants at the next booth blow over onto their sides in this wind, while the cape on a plastic Dracula gets tangled in an arm pointing the way to hot dogs. Nothing about the color of the sky or the force of the wind invites outdoor play.

Back at the front gate, Ms. Cheryl and her boyfriend, Miles, are racing around in matching Frog Fest shirts and plaid shorts, trying to put the final touches on things. With a head of spiky hair and a soul patch on his chin that adds a few years to his baby face, Miles is sixteen years her junior, which makes her a cougar by TV standards, and the age difference has occasionally pulled her up short. At one point this fall, she even called their relationship off, but Miles waited her out, and now they seem like a couple in perfect sync. They motor around the grounds in the Gator Jeeps used by festival staff, checking to see which booths need ice and making sure that the beer ticket window staffers know which color wristband goes with which day. It's a good thing Ms. Cheryl and Miles worked it all out, because he's invaluable today, not just because he is built for the hard physical work required to make a fair happen, but because the heart of a softy beats beneath his burly frame, and he's making sure Ms. Cheryl is supported as much emotionally as physically. The flowers cheering up the trailer she's using as a command post—those are from Miles. No wonder she's still feeling optimistic.

Finally, the gates open, and the crowds can enter. Except, so far, there are no crowds. The skies are less heavily cloud-banked than earlier and the wind has died down, but there is still a hint of chill in the evening air. The sun is setting fast and midway lights come on, stuttering into yellow and orange life. Senior citizens drift through the gate and a few families as well, most heading right for the food. The hub of activity at this moment is the drink ticket area; set just inside the gate, with three windows open at once, this is where the proof-of-age wristbands are sold and tickets are purchased for beer, wine, and cocktails. Despite the small numbers here so far, all three windows are busy.

That, at least, is a good sign. The festival always earns the Chamber between $30,000 and $35,000 after expenses, and beer ticket income is the number-one contributor to its earnings. The actual Chamber budget runs closer to $50,000, so there are a few months every year that the well runs completely dry and the Chamber must operate on credit. Low turnout would not only reduce gate admissions but also yield fewer beer sales, which would leave the Chamber out of cash even sooner.

Chelsea arrives, wearing a warm sweater—not exactly what she envisioned for her festival. She's eager to do her part here, because most of her reign so far has involved representing the festival elsewhere. There have been fewer options for service at home, though she did cut the ribbon at the opening of a medical equipment store in September and helped out with Halloween Fright Fest two weeks ago. It's almost six o'clock, the hour when she will be introduced to fairgoers as their Frog Queen, but she can see her subjects are small in number. Cheryl maintains that she's not concerned: "The night's early, and you can't ever tell whether we're gonna make it on attendance until eight or nine the first night. That's when we'll know."

A faint cry of brass music floats across the fields from a distant site, revealing part of the attendance problem: The rescheduling of the festival has set its opening up against a home game of the Rayne Mighty Wolves. This isn't Texas, but that doesn't mean the townsfolk don't love their football team. The Friday-night lights are illuminating a game that is just getting under way and will hold the attention of a good portion of Rayne's population for a couple of hours yet.

With fewer than a hundred fairgoers gathered in the pavilion, it's time to kick off the festival. Cheryl, Mayor Jimbo, Chamber president Angie Broussard, and all the Frog royalty take the stage. A small band of Boy Scouts and Weeblos, three of each, parades the colors—the Stars and Stripes, the state flag, and the flag of Rayne, which, laden as it is with jamboree ribbons, is larger than the other two. Seeing as the tallest boys tower nearly two feet over their smallest comrades, their march formation is more ragtag than precise, and when they finally halt, half of them stand at ease while the other half are at attention. But just seeing them there, playing their part in the tradition, is a joy. With parents taking photos from one side, the mayor smiling at them from the stage, and the midway behind them pulsing with color, it is a scene Norman Rockwell would have painted.

When she steps forward to introduce herself as "your Rayne Frog Festival Queen," Chelsea is met with applause and a brief burst of camera flashes. From the stage, she scans the small crowd in the pavilion and is relieved that Jace is not one of the few in her audience. It took an act of will for her not to invite him, but she wouldn't put it past him to finally show up for something only after she doesn't want him to.

When she finally gets to leave the stage, she finds herself on the dance floor next to her prom date from a few years before. He's a sweetheart and they haven't really kept in touch the past couple of years, but it's easy enough to talk to him—at least until Jennifer, Chelsea's first runner-up, appears. Though Chelsea and Jennifer were a grade apart in school and not classmates, it's a small town and the dating pool is similarly limited: Chelsea's old date is Jennifer's current boyfriend. The two girls have not interacted since Jennifer lost, and there are plenty of people who still nurse a grudge over that defeat, which both of them know. Jennifer simply ignores Chelsea's presence entirely, and starts talking to the boyfriend. "There I am, in my crown and banner," Chelsea says, "and she just acts like they're alone." Chelsea feels trapped between politeness and not provoking more bitterness in her former rival. When she slips away, she says, "That was like nails on a chalkboard."

The air is actually getting warmer, despite the late hour, and the clouds have parted so that moonlight washes over the slowly building crowds. The musical acts will be starting soon in the pavilion, but for now I follow the ebb and flow of fair-goers checking out the midway. Though the rides are all in motion, the real action is along the lanes serving food and drink. There are plenty of local specialties to be had: "drippy beef" made by the same Crowley family for fifty years, BBQ burgers served up by the Lions Club, and all manner of gumbo. Fittingly, there is more than one booth where you can order frog legs, a delicacy that Miles sums up pretty well: "People say it's just like chicken, but that's not it. It's your basic chicken taste with a little-bitty seafood taste, too."

Because it's a carnival, fried is its own food group. Meat, dough, pickles, candy bars—if you fry it, people will come. A teenage carny, whose paper cap hides her hair but not the supernova of acne swirling on her exposed forehead, dunks Oreos in a vat of pale, sweet batter, then tosses them one at a time into a trough of oil that sizzles when the cookies make contact. She has done this thousands of times, yet she keeps her eyes on what she's doing, concentrating as she swings fat orbs up from the oil and onto a hot metal rack to drain. She slides the cookies in a paper cone and then shakes so much confectioner's sugar onto them that the Oreos resemble snowdrifts. She delivers her handiwork with a grave warning: "Wait three minutes or you'll lose all the skin off the roof of your mouth."

Fairs are no place for discreet consumption. This seems especially true of the alcohol choices around me. A woman built like a Mini Cruiser approaches several friends carrying a slushie pink cocktail in a bowl big enough for a sizable school of goldfish. Her drink contains not only several neon straws but swizzle sticks with streamers, and it takes two hands to hold it. One of her companions sees the drink and scorns it. "You're such a girl!" (Is it still a "girly drink" if it's twenty ounces?) The teasing among her friends doesn't last long—

everyone sips from the cocktail, including the sourpuss who mocked it.

The sky is black, the midway lights blazing in contrast to pure night, when a wave hits. Not a tropical storm, but a wave of people. The game is over—Rayne won!—and with only an hour or two before the gates close, the players, their families, and their fans are turning out in full force. There is no per-hour charge for admission, so the flat entry fee is collected no matter when you arrive; in other words, at the end of the night, the tally won't care whether the festival looked half empty for hours or not. All that it will show is that thousands of people made it after all.

A Cajun band has the crowds filling the dance floor, from little kids hopping around in silly goofball versions of dance steps, to older couples in fine form. The white-haired Golden Frog couple makes a lovely picture, the king gamely wearing his crown, as they hold hands and do-si-do. Soon enough, the dancing spills beyond the pavilion onto the surrounding lawn and into the midway. In the middle of the road, Miles and Ms. Cheryl, who can finally relax and just enjoy the event, are doing a little country swing, laughing as they kick it up. Like a backdrop in a movie about young love, the Ferris wheel rises over them, its lights radiating outward from the star at its center, as it and they spin and spin.

Come morning, things look even better. It's a little chilly in the hour before Frog Derby, but it's already a blue-sky day, and it's supposed to be near eighty by the time of the parade, which means this may be the first rain-free Frog weekend ever. The Frog Derby contestants have gathered in a small function room, and they make for quite a picture. Maddie, Nicole, Summer, and Emily are dressed in the traditional Derby attire, costumes that would challenge the tender psyche of many a high schooler: high-waisted pastel shorts held up by suspenders over checker-cloth blouses, with jaunty caps that serve primarily to draw eyes upward and away from the required sensible grandma shoes. It's about as far from pageant-wear as you can get, but the focus is on tradition, not fashion. In a way, because this getup can make a heavy girl seem heavier and a thin girl look like an old maid, it serves as a great equalizer—it doesn't flatter anyone. The outfit can come off even worse if the girls aren't careful—Ms. Cheryl has to remind them every year that if they choose white shorts, they can't wear colored underwear, or everyone will know.

Their own costumes are only half the equation when it comes to attire. Part of what they are judged on is how well they dress their frogs in little outfits meant to show the girls' creativity. Family members aren't supposed to help make the outfits, but they're more than welcome to help the girls get their frogs dressed, not an easy task. The frogs are often non-compliant (wouldn't you be?), and the outfits are designed like doll clothes, never mind that frog limbs don't conform to doll angles or proportions. Competing sisters Summer and Nicole each clutch a green ward, Summer dressing hers as a cowboy riding a Barbie-sized horse, and Nicole trying to make hers look like a clown, though its head is barely visible through a lime-green marabou fringe. Maddie's frog, Pete, is dressed as an offshore-oil frog, with a canvas jumper that fits him so precisely, it takes not only Maddie but her mother, Monica, and stepdad, Byron, to dress him. Maddie's secret weapon is that Pete's outfit comes with a killer accessory: She has made him a matching oil derrick as well. The final contestant, Emily, has also created an entire identity for her racer: Bella Mae, a farm frog, a little green gal who loves straw hats and wears her hair in braids. As frogs do not actually have hair, Bella Mae's braids are attached to a hat, which she keeps trying to shake off. (The chin-strap doesn't help, as frogs also have no chins.)

Before the judges escort the girls to the pavilion, Bella Mae makes a break for it, hopping out of Emily's grasp and darting away between the legs of contestants. As squeals arise from the girls, Emily does not lead the charge to find her frog—a bad sign for a would-be Frog Derby Queen. Byron scoops Bella Mae up and the Derby troops march off to entertain the waiting crowd.

Frog Derby is many Rayne girls' first chance to be a little celebrity. Not just family and friends come to the Derby, but Visiting Queens, fairgoers who have heard about or witnessed this tradition in the past, and news photographers from all the surrounding towns. A Frog Derby win may imply that other titles lie in a girl's future. Chelsea is living proof: Frog Derby was her first competition; with no interview portion, it was the perfect starter pageant for a girl afraid to speak in public.

The girls lift their frogs out of their buckets and line up behind a velvet rope for press photos, smiling first in one direction and then another, accompanied by the *click click click* of shutters, while their wards' costumed legs dangle plaintively. It is a good ten minutes before the last shutterbug is satisfied and the frogs are returned to their plastic-tub homes, albeit temporarily.

Before a sprawling crowd, the Derby contestants are introduced as they march single-file in a pastel parade before the judges. One at a time, the contestants retrieve their frogs from buckets and set them down on the cement floor. (Unlike in a horse race, distance, not speed, is what matters—the frogs race alone, and there will be no winning by a nose.) Using long slender pointers to encourage them, the girls exhort their green athletes to leap for glory, with men from the local Lions Club on hand to measure how far each frog can get in three hops. Pete changes direction mid-hop, a zigzag that makes it hard to tell how much distance Maddie will get credit for, but he does make it farther than Bella Mae, who has spent all her energy on her earlier breakout attempt and barely musters up a few feet of leapage.

Nicole's unnamed frog earns a cheer from the crowd with its initial leap, an arc that takes it a good two feet high, before a headfirst plunge onto cement. Its forelegs are too short to keep it from doing a face-plant that yields an audible splat sound, meriting a collective groan from viewers. Its remaining hops are much diminished, and it will be Summer's frog who rules the race, each leap longer and more graceful than the last.

As the weary amphibians are returned to their tubs, the local press photographers raise their lenses for the announcement of the winner. Frog-training may be a skill, but creativity takes the day. Summer is third, with Emily—who may have feared her frog but did, after all, make it lovely braids—taking second. When Maddie is crowned as the new Frog Derby Queen, her beaming family is the very vision of team spirit: Dad in his Lions Club vest, Mom in her Frog Festival T-shirt, and Grandpa holding the frog bucket. The outgoing queen is visibly reluctant to pass on the crown, which is nearly as tall as Chelsea's, graced with a greener frog. Maddie doesn't have enough hands for all the spoils of victory: a bouquet of roses, a trophy nearly the length of her torso, and poor, long-suffering Pete. She keeps the loot and Grandpa takes the frog.

During Derby, Chelsea is busy on the far side of the pavilion performing one of her definitive duties as Frog Queen: posing for portraits with a frog the size of a softball. Other queens line up to have their pictures taken with her and her frog, or with one of their own. Chelsea shows the visitors the ropes: To hold a frog right, you have to find its backbone, which is as thick as a pencil, and pinch your thumb and forefinger on either side, while supporting the weight of the frog with your other palm. This position keeps the frog stable and less likely to jump out of your hand, though it won't help if you're squeamish about touching something cold and wet and a little sticky.

The photographers call out instructions and, for a moment, it's like a shoot on *America's Next Top Model.* "Chelsea, hold it up higher!" "Chelsea, over here!" "Look over your shoulder!" And, inevitably, "Kiss it!" There is no point running for Frog Queen if you won't kiss a frog, as Chelsea knows. She makes a show of complying, holding the frog up to her face while looking at the camera, but she actually keeps the green beast a hairsbreadth away from her lips. She's going to have to do this pose a lot, and there's no way she's going to let her lips linger on wet frog skin all morning long.

Usually that's enough, but this year, the photographers want more variety. As Chelsea starts to leave the pavilion, one follows her. "Wait! I want to get you eating frog legs!" Chelsea is not thrilled with the idea of being photographed chewing, but she knows her job and agrees, dragging her Teen Queen along for the picture. Standing beneath Budweiser banners and a hand-painted Jaycees sign, each girl holds a hot batter-crusted frog leg nearly the length of a ruler, and waits for the click. "No, a real bite," the photographer says, and the girls oblige by locking white teeth around crunchy ends. "You're still *holding* it, not eating it," he complains. He doesn't understand that festival queens all know the golden rule of photography: Never break your smile. No matter what is said to you, no matter how anyone tries to get you to relax into a more casual pose, keep your smile perfect, because that photo of you will be around when you are not, and it will stand in for your festival as well. His entreaties are for naught, but he can't help himself. "C'mon, eat more!"

As soon as he's gone, Chelsea puts the frog leg down. She doesn't have anything against frog legs, but what she really wants is one of the moist and sloppy BBQ burgers at the next booth. She needs to eat something so that she doesn't faint in the heat of the parade, which she has to get dressed for soon.

One of the virtues of having an RV park is that Rayne is perfectly equipped for families who want to camp out during the festival weekend. Camping in this case does not mean a tent and a fire for your s'mores; it means a snug homelette on wheels, tricked out with a sleeping nook, a banquette that serves as a living room, and a counter that acts as a kitchen. The parking lot is full of campers today, RVs set up in rows with just enough space between to allow for the concrete version of yards, complete with lawn chairs and grills or roasting pits. Despite living in town, Chelsea's family has a camper set up so that she can be close to the fairgrounds for the entire weekend. A good queen should be omnipresent at her own festival.

Chelsea's mom, Vicki, tells me to come on in, and I'm glad to be out of the midday sun, which is coming on like a bully. Yesterday's worries about the lower temperatures have evaporated, baked away by a day that thinks it's still summer. It'll be a relief for Chelsea to take off the wool sweater she has worn all morning, and she slips into the tiny stall-sized bathroom to change into an outfit both less warm and more glamorous.

Sipping diet soda in the cool camper, Vicki talks about the queen preparing herself on the other side of the narrow door. Even a few years ago, she never would've pictured her daughter leading a parade, so this weekend is a thrill for mother and child alike. "She wanted this so much and she worked so hard for it," Vicki says. It's not the position of honor itself but Chelsea's dedication that puts a note of emotion in Vicki's soft, lilting voice. "She's a good girl. As a parent, what more can you ask?"

The bathroom door opens and Chelsea steps out, transformed. Her dark hair falls loose to her pale shoulders, bare in a sleeveless white evening gown. Jewels dot the fitted bodice, which hugs her waist above a waterfall of silk that pools on the linoleum at her feet. Sun streams in through the bathroom window, transforming the simplest confines into something magical: The glass shower door glows luminescent white, framing her like an icon on a lit votive. But there's no time to dawdle; she needs to finish getting dressed. "Mama, can you zip me?"

Where else but Louisiana can a girl in an eighteen-inch crown, rhinestone-studded velvet banner, evening gown, and four-inch heels emerge from an RV without anyone batting an eyelash? Chelsea steps carefully down the metal-grate steps and holds up her train to thread her way through the parking lot. As her mom helps Chelsea make her way to the family pickup truck, Chelsea says that the first night of the festival had seemed perfect once the crowds finally started pouring in. "I was so happy seeing all of those people—even all the drunk ones!"

Her dad steers the truck toward the staging area for the parade, passing by the storefronts along South Adams, where "old school" and "the latest thing" rub shoulders, or, in this case, face each other down from across the street. Farmer's True Value Hardware sits directly opposite the Glamour Closet boutique, making this perhaps the only block on earth where you can buy both an industrial-sized canister of Overnite Ant & Roach Killer *and* a really cute gold lamé handbag. Just off Depot Square, a barista with an eye-ring peers out the door of Java Junkie; at the opposite end of the square, women three or four times her age tend the register at Worthmore 5 & 10, a true five-and-dime store, its front window crowded with plastic reindeer faded from too many seasons in the sun and a Santa whose chipped-paint lips part in a permanent, soundless ho ho ho.

At the staging area, Ms. Cheryl and Miles weave between the floats and bands lining up for blocks, giving instructions and steering marchers in the right direction. Ms. Cheryl is in high spirits—the weather never got worse than chilly yesterday, attendance not only held but is rising with each event, and the streets are lined with people ready for a parade. (Miles is in high spirits, too, because a happy Cheryl makes a happy Miles—plus, it's just damn fun to drive a Gator everywhere.) The model of unflappability, Ms. Cheryl answers a question that has come over her walkie-talkie, while simultaneously steering a Visiting Queen toward the royalty float.

Frog's new date has somewhat limited the attendance of visiting queens, who had to choose between this and other festivals already scheduled for this weekend. Brandy and Kristen will both be at the swell Orange Ball, a half hour's drive from their hometown, as will Lauren, because Orange is the home festival of one of her dearest Rhinestone Sisters. Of queens who make it to Frog, the majority ride on a flatbed trailer set aside for visiting royalty, while a few come with their own wheels (which is more the tradition in other states). The Gueydan Duck Queen graces an enormous decoy of her namesake waterfowl, which would be eye-catching enough even without the burly male mascot riding in the bed of the 4×4 pulling her float. With an oversized feathered head and cloth wings that fan out, the mascot aims hard for cute—but its body is cloaked in a heavy dark robe and its wings end in thick black gloves, creating a sinister undertone: Daffy as Serial Killer.

Chelsea climbs aboard the top level of the Frog royalty float, trying not to snag her gown on a sliver of painted wood. Her mom follows to help get her situated in the green-and-gold box seat she will share with her Teen Queen, Kelsey. First, they position half her velvet train beneath her and then arrange the rest so that it swirls around her feet (her *own* feet, and this time intentionally). Though there is a wall rising up behind her in the box, the shape of Chelsea's frog mantle prohibits her from actually sitting back, so she must maintain perfectly erect posture for the next two hours. In some states, queen floats have harnesses or standing braces to keep them from pitching off into traffic should the route get bumpy or the float pull up short, but this is not the norm in Louisiana. Chelsea will have to maintain her steadiness in all this gear through sheer will.

Kelsey climbs up to join Chelsea and sits on the other side

of a laundry-sized wicker basket full of swag for the crowd. Chelsea discovered a Web site that sold Mardi Gras beads studded with dangling miniature frogs, the perfect throws for this parade, and ordered dozens of packages. She's excited to show Kelsey the strands—until she realizes that all the frog legs have ended up knit together, beads and webbed toes now forming stubborn clumps. The two queens start untangling the beads—a task that seems increasingly impossible—as Ms. Cheryl passes the word that it's time to get this rolling party started.

With a jolt, the float starts to move and Chelsea's heart beats faster. After so many years on the sidewalk looking up as queens roll by, she has swapped spots: She's the one waving; she's the one smiling down at the little girls with stars in their eyes.

Tonight she will see the Frog Festival draw the biggest crowds in its history, so many fairgoers that the interstate will get backed up and police will have to reroute traffic. This turnout means that, for the first time ever, the Chamber of Commerce will have enough funds for its entire year without needing a line of credit. Early tomorrow she will join the mayor and his wife, and all the Chamber of Commerce honchos, for breakfast with Percy Sledge, the mainstage headliner. Then she and Kelsey will don eye-popping matching frog-print jumpers for Sunday Frog Mass. Later still, after the frog races are over, the last band has packed up its amps, and the Ferris wheel has stopped turning, she will finally turn on her phone and unblock Jace, discovering that her silence has, too late, prompted him to show some emotion. The inevitable tearful breakup will come on Monday.

But at this particular moment, all Chelsea can see is a tableau of cheering throngs flanking the streets, thousands upon thousands of Frog revelers basking in the sunlight that warms their upturned faces. There's not a cloud in sight.

11

Heavy the Head

With Thanksgiving past, red-and-green holiday decorations have appeared in seemingly every shop window. While the countless tinseled harbingers announce a cheery season, Lauren's crown has gotten heavier. Her festival board has added the weight of a decision to her already overcrowded life: They would like her to boycott Queen of Queens. But they're also not going to *make* her do so. In theory, letting her choose whether to participate or not gives her power over the situation. That is meant to be a kindness, but it doesn't feel that way to her.

Just three years since Rita wiped out Cameron Parish, Ike has scrubbed the landscape of trees, shrubs, homes, schools, anything that dared rise since the last purge. There is no way Fur is going to send its crew to the Louisiana Association of Fairs and Festivals Convention, which hosts Queen of Queens. Fur wants to send a message to LAFF: Festivals need resources, not parties. Yet as principled as this stance may be, it may make no waves at all. It is possible no other festivals will follow suit, leaving lonely Fur to tilt at windmills.

LAFF is an organization that makes the strength of the festival tradition possible, fostering both the quality and longevity of these events. At the same time, LAFF is like any other institution run by human beings: Even good people doing valuable things can make judgments that other good people will question. Fur's gripe with LAFF is not small. When Katrina and then Rita devastated swaths of southern Louisiana, leaving thousands homeless and their communities destroyed, LAFF nonetheless held its full-on convention just three months later, a three-day affair involving parties, dinners, musical performances, and the Queen of Queens pageant. Some member festivals found the undimmed nature of festivities—the many thousands of dollars spent on ballrooms and bands—inappropriate. And now it's happening again.

Though the board members are boycotting the event, they have stopped short of saying that Lauren *must* play along. The board is grateful that she has agreed to spend another year traveling so far and so frequently, and know that her costs will eventually outstrip the meager income provided. Ms. Vicki also understands that for a girl on her last title, as Lauren is, Queen of Queens is both a final shot at competition and a precious valedictory lap, likely the only time she'll ever be with all her Rhinestone Sisters. With all that in mind, the Fur board has left the decision up to Lauren, saying it will support whatever she decides to do.

Lauren supports Fur's message to LAFF, but she's also competitive by nature and was looking forward to Queens of Queens. She placed in the Top 15 as Cattle Queen and would love to go back and have a chance to place even higher. This is not an effortless call to make.

Her decision still weighs on her mind this December morning as she waits in a Lake Charles parking lot, ready to act as a good host queen. With the festival canceled, Lauren has instead asked Chelsea, Brandy, and Kristen to come see where Fur would have been held—and why it won't be. She can help get the word out about what happened here by making the devastation real for girls who represent relatively untouched parts of the state. Though Ms. Vicki has helped her make arrangements, this is not a miniature version of the Fur Festival, but a day of learning and service.

Right after Ike, Lauren had wanted to do some sort of fund-raiser for Fur, using her profile as queen and her deep well of personal energy to pull something together on short notice. But Ms. Vicki had pointed out that the most pressing needs were not monetary; Fur still had the funds once budgeted for that year's festival. A well-meant fund-raiser wouldn't actually repair roads or rebuild the entire school system or make people less homeless. "Her exact words were, 'People need to see the Fur Queen,'" Lauren says. "She told me what they really needed from me was to be out there saying that we're not going away, that we'll all get through this." To that end, Lauren spent yesterday in the makeshift schools where Cameron's students finished out their semester. Joined by Miss Cameron, Lauren read books, talked to the children, and let them try on her crown. "Even the boys wanted to wear it," she says. "We told them it could be a king's crown or whatever they wanted it to be!"

Today, with this handful of Visiting Queens, she can make a good impression for Fur in a different way. The girls have an 8:30 A.M. appointment to volunteer at a women's shelter. Community service is one of the staples of festival queen life, from the Bayou Teche Bear Queen doing forestry education to the Sulfur Heritage Queen cutting off ten inches of her hair to donate to cancer victims. The Erath 4th of July Queen is so busy with volunteer service projects, especially on behalf of the armed forces, that getting to pageants and festivals takes a backseat.

Brandy pulls in, relieved and annoyed. She'd worked up until closing at Cane's last night, so yesterday was a full and exhausting day for her. Because this shelter is four hours from LaPlace, that means she had to get up at 4:30 A.M., on less than five hours' sleep, and drive alone through the dark of predawn hours. That was an unnerving prospect for two reasons: A thick fog has blanketed half the state the last few mornings, making driving dangerous, and today's headlines are all about the serial murders of seven young women in a parish through which she had to drive. She's relieved to have made it safely, but still annoyed by the fact that she didn't expect to make this drive alone.

Kristen and Brandy were supposed to carpool today. Having a companion would have made the early hour more palatable and the whole enterprise safer. But Kristen changed her mind yesterday—casually, or so it seemed to Brandy—saying she had decided to spend the night in Baton Rouge with Chance. That put her an hour and a half closer to the shelter, so her own trip would be shorter and she could get up later. But she also left Brandy on her own and steaming.

Gamely tamping down her irritation, Brandy focuses on the task at hand. One of her grandmothers died just after Thanksgiving, a loss still so fresh that the mention of it makes Brandy's brown eyes well with tears. On Thanksgiving Day, the family usually went to the grandmother's house. This year, all the fixings—gumbo, sweet tea, cookies—had already been prepared before Grandma got sick and couldn't host. A week later she was gone. "It was so hard," Brandy says, "seeing everything there without her." It wasn't easy to enter her house surrounded by so many poignant reminders, like the heights of all the grandchildren still written on the wall. Turning grief into action, Brandy has brought large bags of Grandma's clothing with her to this shelter, which happens to be in the town where Grandma once lived. It feels right to Brandy that these things should have a homecoming. "She was a schoolteacher here, so this is like her continuing to help out the place where she was from."

Chelsea pulls in and greets the other girls, excited that it is only a small group today. She hasn't seen any of them since Yam, and it'll be nice to spend time with them without getting lost in the crowd. Chelsea loves the fact that being a queen provides good volunteer opportunities, and after only a few months, she is developing a sense of propriety about the dual role of queen and volunteer. When she did the Down

syndrome walkathon, wearing crown and banner seemed perfectly natural for such a paradelike event. But she couldn't say
the same a few weeks back, when she delivered Thanksgiving
baskets.

Canned goods and nonperishables are collected town-
wide in Rayne and then assembled into food baskets for the
town's poor, a tradition familiar to people all over the country. The day that Thanksgiving baskets were to be delivered,
Chelsea had a theater class she couldn't afford to miss. Her
group's final project, a Louisiana version of *A Midsummer
Night's Dream,* was due to be performed in class at the same
time the baskets would be going out in Rayne. If she skipped
the class, she worried about "looking all self-centered, focused
just on what I needed instead of my group," but there was
no question about the importance of the baskets: The Frog
Queen simply can't miss out. It took "serious butt-kissing,"
but she persuaded her group to let her work only behind the
scenes, preparing the play but not showing up for it.

To her dismay, after all her negotiations, when she got back
to Rayne, not only were all the baskets assembled, but the
Lions Club was doing most of the delivering without the
town's queens. Instead, all the royalty, and many of their moms,
were going together to deliver the same basket to one house.
Chelsea had a funny feeling about this—what it would be like
to have all these people show up on your doorstep at once.
Ms. Cheryl had a similar concern, and when they arrived at the
home of the intended recipient, she went ahead alone, and
warned the woman about the size of the entourage. Chelsea

describes the scene: "The woman comes out in her pajamas and slippers and picks up the basket, and just looks at us. 'I didn't expect so many,' she whispered." Chelsea felt for the woman, whose discomfort wasn't universally noticed. "Some of the moms were saying, 'Can we get a picture? Can we get a picture?' " So there the woman stood, in her bedclothes, willed into being evidence of good deeds for the scrapbooks of strangers. Chelsea was horrified. "I still think about it and cringe. I just feel like whenever we're doing that kind of community work, we shouldn't have the crowns on our heads."

Today she gets it her way: In T-shirts and jeans and sneakers, they're queens incognito. But one is also queen in absentia, at least for the moment: Kristen texts Brandy to say that she ended up sick with a migraine last night and can't make it to the shelter. If she feels better, she'll try to meet her fellow queens at lunchtime. Brandy relays this information with one eyebrow firmly raised. Still stung by being ditched, she manages to say "migraine" in a tone that provides its own air quotes, and Lauren wonders if "migraine" means "I stayed out too late last night."

Whether or not it's the primary issue this morning, Kristen really has been knocked back by migraines lately. Migraines have been part of her life since third grade, and for years prescription remedies have kept her symptoms in check. But now, just as her life is busiest with school and Cattle duties, the migraines have started outpacing the medication by a long shot. Coming two or three times a week, the headaches make her throw up and lay her out cold for a day at a time. Some weeks, she misses classes, and other times she's forced to cut short her Visiting Queen trips; in bad weeks, both. Her doctor prescribed a new medication—this time a strong antidepressant—but its virtues (the headache disappears in short order) were outmatched by its flaws (Kristen was unconscious all day as a result). When she called to make a follow-up appointment, her doctor said he couldn't see her till February. Since then, she's been limping along, choosing between less-effective remedies or losing whole days curled up in a ball in a dark room. But the girls don't know all this: They only see her absence from the shelter. Coupled with her not giving Brandy a ride, it has made them start to doubt her reliability.

The three girls head inside the shelter, where they are met by volunteer coordinator Sallye LeBleu. Lauren, taking the lead as the host queen, introduces herself first, and the others follow suit, but it is Sallye who dominates the room. Tall, with short blond hair becoming salt-and-pepper, Sallye is a striking mix of warmth and confidence. It is easy to imagine the Air Force officer she once was as she strides ahead, leading the queens past a cozy living room, a pantry, and a kitchen, where meals are prepared for the thirty-three women and children staying here. She tells the girls that she understands her clients well, having herself suffered domestic abuse when she was a young woman, just as her mother had suffered before her. The girls are surprised that this take-charge professional was once a battered woman; they can't envision someone so strong ever being pushed around.

Sallye leads the girls into the sunny children's room, a

space clean and bright, dominated by a decorated Christmas tree. The fake fir is crowned not with a star but by a topper in the shape of a house and globe, with a banner reading, "Peace on Earth Begins at Home." Festooning the tree are stiff ribbons bearing slogans like "Hands Are Not for Hitting," sobering invocations of domestic violence amid the festivity.

The children's room is silent as the queens take in Sallye's description of the need for places like this shelter. "By bedtime tonight, four more women will be dead from domestic violence," she tells them. Despite such statistics, when Sallye goes to police academies and sheriff's offices to offer training, she is sometimes met with resistance. One sheriff said to her, "Why do we need training? We ain't got any of that stuff down here."

She shakes her head at such wisdom and reminds the girls of the headlines that morning about the establishment of a task force to investigate the serial murders. Body after body has been dumped in publicly accessible areas in Jefferson Davis Parish in the past three years. But concern of a serial predator didn't really take hold until the pace picked up: Just weeks after the sixth victim was found, a seventeen-year-old girl, the youngest yet, went missing as well. Even then, the sheriff's office seemed intent on playing up the victims' "high-risk" lifestyle: Some were drug users, some had rap sheets, one had been a prostitute, and all were poor. That each one was a real person, someone's sister or daughter, and, in three cases, someone's mother, didn't seem to get as much attention; it was as if there were a tacit agreement that as long as these women remained on the other side of the tracks in the public's imagination, the story could feel safely distant. But they lived real lives at the same time as their fellow Louisiana girls in this room, so full remove is impossible.

When Sallye leaves the girls to their first task, cleaning the children's room and sorting out its broken toys and books, the queens are happy for a release from the heaviness of the conversation, but it still weighs on them, and they work silently until Brandy's phone rings from across the room, where it is buried in her bag. She waits it out and it falls silent, then rings again. After a slightly longer pause this time, it rings once more, until she finally digs the phone out and looks at the screen. Just as she expected, it is Cane's calling, but she doesn't answer; she trained her crew well, got the store ready before she left last night, and now it's up to them to prove they can handle a shift without her. She turns the phone off and goes back to a pile of blocks.

When Sallye returns, she invites the girls into the women's living quarters to perform one of the million mundane tasks that is required to keep a shelter going. Today's task is as dull and practical as can be. The girls are going to replace dozens of doorknobs and dresser drawer pulls throughout the living quarters. It might not take them more than an hour or so, but that's an hour the social workers and advocates won't have to steal from their caseloads.

The queens are surprised at the initial normalcy of the scene inside the living quarters. In the first of three rooms, Sallye introduces them not as queens but just as volunteers there to do some work, and then leaves them to it. Brandy feels "relief to see the women and children looking just fine, the kids still playing like kids." Lauren had silently nursed fears of "seeing black, swollen eyes," but instead, "There's the cutest little boy ever. You'd never guess he was in a bad situation—it doesn't look like, 'Hey, I'm in a shelter because I'm abused.'"

The work goes quickly and easily, though in the second room, as they work on the dressers, Chelsea is again mindful that other's people lives and emotions are involved. The hardware for the drawer pulls requires them to slide each drawer out. "It's kind of awkward because we want to respect boundaries," she says, "yet we're opening their drawers."

In the third room, Brandy is set upon by two kids who are pretending to be puppies and want to lick her, and she tries to be a good sport. Chelsea is focused on the kids' mom, who looks the same age as the queens, if not younger. While the mother talks about trying to find a home for the three of them, Chelsea wonders, "How do you take that on?"

When the last knob has been screwed into place, the girls return to the children's room, where Sallye thanks them for their time and work. She asks them to carry their experience today with them, helping others understand both what women face and what they should not have to accept. "As festival queens," she reminds them, "you have a sphere of influence. You're role models—you need to show what strong women can do." Then she ushers them out into the sunlight.

The girls decide that it would be more fun to ride all together now than to travel in separate cars. We're in Lauren's territory and she drives confidently toward her domain, despite her anxiety about what she'll find. It's a half hour to the town of Cameron, the seat of the parish that shares its name, and the city feel of Lake Charles gives way to country almost immediately. Lauren steers us through Cameron Prairie, where few buildings interrupt the landscape of fields and wetlands punctuated by low trees and small herds of cattle. Soon, the fields are cut through with muddy canals, their banks dotted with sun-worshipping alligators, slender and dark, skin as thick and corrugated as strips of rubber flung from the tires of an eighteen-wheeler. As the territory gives way entirely to marshland, yard-high reeds plush with egrets and glossy onyx blackjacks, I comment on the loveliness of our surroundings. Lauren's voice is thick with pride. "I know, right. We have it all here."

As we drive through the marsh known as the Big Burns, the sky is steel blue, not dark exactly, but not electric or bright, either. Turtles bob in the water, birds swoop in and out of the reeds, and the canals are ripe with bounty for the men in T-shirts who stand on the banks with crab nets in hand. Chelsea is a little jealous of them. "I've never been crabbing. Or hunting, for that matter. My family won't let me shoot a gun."

"First time I ever shot a gun was at my festival," says Lauren. "I did skeet shooting as queen and I hit every single one . . ." She waits a beat. "On the ground!"

Brandy doesn't hunt but she'd like to try—she wonders aloud why she's never met a guy who does that sort of thing.

"Why can't I ever find a boyfriend who mud-rides, hunts, and fishes? I'd be game!"

Kristen is on her way here, too, but she enjoys her ride less. Medicated and feeling better, she's determined to meet us for lunch but regrets traveling alone. For miles and miles, her gas light has been on. It's been a half hour since she got off the highway and left behind all semblances of cities or towns. The road into the heart of the parish is long and slender, two lanes with almost no shoulder between the cars and the canals, and there have been no gas stations, no signs pointing to rest stops, just her and her car and plenty of reasons not to pull over: Without a breakdown lane, her little Saturn could be wiped out by a speeding truck; all alone, a five-foot-two girl would make an easy target for a man with bad intentions; and, well, *alligators*. Crying, she calls her best friend, Amber, and begs her to stay on the phone until, at long last, a gas station finally comes into view.

When she pulls into the parking lot of the roadside lunch spot where the others already wait, she gushes with relief. "You have *no* idea!" It hasn't been a banner day all around. Chance, in her words, "is being an asshole." She wants him to meet her back at her family's place in LaPlace tomorrow, but he's preemptively begging off. He still hasn't been to her house and she can't understand why. "You'll be there," she said when they last spoke, and he refused to answer. And now he's ducking her calls. "He thinks that I'll put up with that?" Her eyes flash. "Oh, *hell* no." But then she backtracks, the bravado gone. "Whatever. We fight. It blows over."

Things do not thaw immediately between queens over lunch, but the girls are given time to warm up as they listen to Fur Festival board members Ryan King and Ms. Vicki talk about Ike. Storms the size of Ike are known in these parts as "hundred-year storms," because of their statistical rarity. But Cameron has now suffered hits from three in just over fifty years: Audrey (in 1957), and then Rita and Ike. Only one town building survived all three: the Roosevelt-era Cameron Courthouse. Rita was so bad that the town's population dropped from over 10,000 to under 6,000, and in the intervening three years, it has rebounded only to 8,500. Many of the repairs have still not been completed, with insurers making it so onerous for homeowners to file claims that some have just given up trying. And now it's back to square one. Ms. Vicki shakes her head. "Ike coming so close after Rita has really put a damper on rebuilding," she says. "Who knows when it'll happen?"

Ryan quotes Roland Primo, the fiftieth King Fur: "It took forty-eight years after Audrey for Cameron to look like it did. It'll be decades again." That's a reality even a local like Ryan can't ignore; he's had to move his wife and kids out of Cameron twice in three years, and this time they're not moving back. Retreating from his hometown is painful for someone whose family's roots run so deep here.

In fact, Ryan's dad is one of the men who've helped provide the raw materials for one of the festival's most unique traditions: Each new queen receives (and keeps) a custom-designed fur coat made from Cameron Parish pelts (mostly nutria, the Louisiana mink). This is an unparalleled luxury for a festival queen, a big added incentive for girls who consider competing here, but a detail that only the most brazen queen would admit to thinking about. Ryan points out the window and notes that his dad trapped one year's nutria just a half mile away from the table where we're sitting.

"You girls wanna know what Lauren said right after we crowned her?" he asks. Of course, they all do, and Lauren puts down her sandwich, wondering what mortifying thing he is about to reveal. "I asked her, 'Why'd you come all this way to run?'" He has a captive audience, Lauren included. "And she says, 'For the jacket!'"

Everyone laughs, but Lauren's cheeks flush a little, and her eyes are slightly narrower than they would be from mirth alone. Knowing how a story like that would sound on the Voy boards, she hopes that the girls here have already seen ample evidence that she's not that shallow. But she's a good sport and so plays along. "Well, I waited till *after* I won to tell you, so that means you got yourself a smart queen!" By the time the meal ends, laughter has replaced tension, and harmony between the girls seems restored.

The lunch café sits just beyond the edge of Cameron proper, and bears no hint of the recent storm's fury. The closer to Cameron center that one gets, however, the worse things look. A rolled-over mobile home sits right where it landed in a canal, water ebbing in and out of metal siding now in ribbons. Lot to lot, front walls of homes are peeled away carelessly like wrapping paper, exposing soaked bedroom sets and living rooms where branches rest atop La-Z-Boys. The images are disheartening, especially for Lauren, who can picture what it looked like before. She had spent a lot of time watching the news when Ike blew in, trying to see if she could tell how far and how fast the water had risen, but she hasn't actually visited Cameron since the storm. Nothing prepared her for this. "I'm blown away at all this damage even after months. It breaks my heart to see so many of the homes ripped into shreds."

The wind and water have lifted houses off their foundations, dropping some on other people's properties entirely. The displacement has led to a homely categorization system for disaster relief officials: On the front of the trailers, the owners' names have been spray-painted in big letters, along with the address of where the home should be sitting, as opposed to where it sits now. On one trailer, someone has added a big black frowny-face symbol, and another has written in orange scrawl, "Please help us!" Whoever left these poignant messages is long gone—this country lane, once home to hundreds, feels deserted. The only motion in the landscape comes from a tilted house, where thin strands of siding bob on the wind and the loose front door tries to slam itself shut only to bounce open off a limb that has fallen across the doorstep. Pale floral curtains flutter half inside, half outside what once was a kitchen window.

Brandy murmurs, "They don't show this on TV. It's like nothing happened here. But it did."

A few miles on, homes that have been reclaimed start coming into view, pickup trucks in the driveway, clothes on clotheslines. There are untouched houses here as well, raised up on stilts eight to twelve feet off the ground, which identifies them as having been built since Rita, when the parish changed its regulations in hopes of lessening the devastation of future hurricanes. It's a policy that seems to have worked for many buildings, one of which is emblazoned with a cheeky sign: CAJUN HIGH RISE.

We pull into the parking lot of a motel undergoing repairs, its wooden facade badly battered. As we step out of the car, Lauren points across the road and we follow her indication— of nothing. At a glance there is little to see there but scrubby grass beneath gray sky. "That's the Fur Festival," she says, and we cross the street to see what once was.

The festival and pageant both used to be held on the Cameron School grounds, a cluster of buildings that formed the epicenter of town life. Rita wiped them all away, leaving nothing but their concrete footprints behind, and, in time, weeds have encroached upon even those. A new school, housing all the grades, had to be built, and on another parcel entirely, but when the festival returned, it was a matter of pride that the old school grounds were now maintained as pallets for all the outdoor Fur events. Now even those remnants are distressed, and the land is studded with debris. As we walk down the still-defined aisle of the auditorium where decades of queens were crowned, I wonder if any of them could have imagined that someday the sturdy brick scene of their triumph would simply blow away. No wonder the board wants their current Fur Queen to be visible; she's the only part of her kingdom left standing.

Back in Lake Charles, after the sun sets, the girls are glad to just sit for a while, ensconced in an Olive Garden booth, taking respite after a twelve-hour day that involved confronting the subject of violence and witnessing the devastation of an Ike-smashed community. "I could use a drink," says Lauren, and Brandy agrees. Both are of legal age to do just that if they wish, but the subject of drinking is tricky for queens. The law may ban drinking under twenty-one, but festival rules prohibit drinking when you have your crown or banner on, *regardless* of age. Tonight, even with their crowns stowed away, they all order tea or diet soda instead.

"You have to be careful about drinking, going out," Chelsea says. Though only twenty, she drinks socially in very limited quantities. "Everyone has a personal life, but that's only when you take off your crown. As long as a queen isn't going around saying, 'Do this, drink underage,' I think it's okay."

"Everybody drinks," Lauren says. "It's Louisiana."

"Yeah, but everybody talks, too," counters Kristen. "You know everyone's watching."

This brings up Sallye's "sphere of influence" comment, about which Lauren offers a surprising analysis: "To be perfectly honest, I don't think about it like that. I am doing a job for the parish and I try to do that well, but I'm supposed to make you think about the *festival*—I don't worry about whether anyone is looking up to *me*."

Brandy wonders, "But can you really avoid it? I mean, we're in these positions. . . ."

Chelsea considers both takes. "I guess being Frog Queen gives me more of an invitation to represent things that are important to me, like the Down syndrome walk, but before this, I hadn't thought of children looking up to me exactly. I did see that at the Christmas parade when all the little boys ran up to Santa—"

"But the girls ran up to you, right?" Kristen finishes Chelsea's sentence. "Same thing in Abbeville for me."

Lauren qualifies her earlier assessment, pretending exasperation. "I never said we weren't role models, just that I don't like to *think* about it!" And they all laugh. Plates of pasta sit half eaten, and tall tumblers of iced tea and diet Coke grow warm, beads of sweat forming on clear glass as the girls discuss how it feels to be in the public eye. They all agree that it's gotten harder in the last few years, now that their biggest critics have online forums on which to attack them.

Chelsea looks down at her water glass, as if sizing it up. "I guess in a sense that all these stories on the Voy boards are driving me to do better at Queen of Queens." She knows that the supporters of the girl she beat, the girl whose year this was supposed to be, will be waiting for her to blow it and will be jubilant if she does. Brandy, also having defeated the

186 DAVID VALDES GREENWOOD

favorite at Cotton, is in the same boat, only worse, since she's an outsider. But she isn't planning to read the Voy boards any-time soon. "I don't care to know what others think. I have enough to worry about."

"It's stupid anyway," Lauren grouses. "Why do people keep this stuff going, months after it's over? I say, 'Don't take competition outside the pageant.' " But this is wishful think-ing. As representatives of four of the most prominent titles in the state, they are prime targets and they know it. This is especially true as D.C. Mardi Gras and Queen of Queens approach.

No wonder Chelsea admits, "I'm nervous. It's my first time for both." But she won't be alone at either event: Since her mom doesn't fly, Brooke and another former Frog Queen, Charmaine Landry, are planning to travel to D.C. to support Chelsea, making sure she knows what she's supposed to do, as well as helping with hair and makeup. Less formally, both will also have her back at Queen of Queens, where each com-peted multiple times, between them netting several of the coveted red pins. With these women on her side, she's at least not flying blind. "So I'm like, 'Well, let's try to go for it,' but I honestly don't know what to expect."

Having now spent months among these four girls, I don't know, either. If Queen of Queens crowns another unvarnished natural like current titleholder Brandi, that favors Kristen. But if a more obviously polished queen appeals to judges at this level, that would mean Brandy or Lauren. And though Chelsea's shyness might hurt in competition against others who are more outgoing, she's already proved that she can rock a closed-door interview.

I ask the question directly, knowing that this is a query most festival queens evade out of a sense of propriety. "Okay, so who's a contender to win?"

"Me!" Only Brandy answers immediately, and she *tries* to sound firm, but then admits that she has been practicing that answer on the advice of Ms. Nicky, a well-known pageant coach and judge (and also Lauren's boss at Head to Toe boutique). "She told me that I have to be able to say that or I won't believe it myself, and if I don't, the judges won't." The trick, of course, is getting to a point where Brandy doesn't feel a little embarrassed and apologetic for answering that way.

Chelsea is less sanguine. "Honestly, the judges don't know me. And it sucks, 'cause you're up against eighty girls."

Kristen laughs a husky laugh. "Yep, it's pretty much a crapshoot." Of course, no one thought she'd win Cattle, either.

Lauren says nothing, listening to her friends talk about their chances. Normally, she'd be right in there with Brandy, talking a good game, ready to take on all comers. She has no doubt about her own skill, and she's more ready to compete this one last time than she ever was before. But she has made her decision—or, more accurately, she has returned the decision to her festival, making the board do the hard work for itself.

"They told me to decide but I wouldn't. So I said to Ms. Vicki, 'You're my festival. *You* tell *me* what you need.'" She knew what the answer would be, what it *had* to be: Don't go. She completely gets it and, still, it feels like a loss. Nevertheless, like a good queen, she puts the best face on things. Smiling across the table at the others, she admonishes them, "Y'all better kick butt for me."

DRAMA SEASON

You can't be timid
and be a girl in this world.

> —Pam Vest,
>   mother of Paige Vest,
>   the last Utica Ice Cream Festival Queen

12

We Interrupt This Festival Season . . .

Winter comes, such as it does in Louisiana—a chill in the air, some gray skies, maybe a sweater is in order. This year snow falls once, a tiny amount destined to last a day, so magical and rare an event that YouTube is suddenly full of home movies in which the front hoods of cars appear as beignets dusted in powdered sugar at Café du Monde. Nature has at last provided something to enjoy, not fear.

As the days grow shorter, the festival calendar dims. In December or January, almost no queens join the sisterhood, save for the holiday titlists, like Christmas on the Bayou and Miss Merry Christmas. Queen mailboxes fill with cards from their sisters around the state, but are near empty of invites and will stay that way until well after the New Year. (This is even more true with the cancellation of Fur, a January event.) A queen's royal duties are likely to be limited to her own town during this season, when her energies are mostly expended on family and friends.

Christmas morning finds Brandy and her siblings ripping

bows off select gifts labeled as coming from Santa. She spends the next few hours helping her mom cook family specialties, broccoli with cheese and sweet-potato crunch, for lunch at the home of Brandy's "Mimi," her surviving grandmother. At Mimi's house, the presents not from Santa are unwrapped, and many of Brandy's are Cotton-themed, just as she'd hoped.

Similarly, Chelsea is being showered with frogabilia. She had wanted to do an all-frog Christmas tree, but her mom put a kibosh on that idea. "She has a thing that it has to be a green tree," Chelsea says, "and a bunch of frogs won't show up." Even so, Chelsea receives six new frog ornaments this morning, permanent mementos of this magic year that is already passing. The morning unfolds as it always does: Her uncle tries to earn laughs by making what he calls his "cowboy" face, which involves taking out his teeth and bizarrely mis-shaping his own jaw; her aunt restores propriety, focusing attention on the presents, enforcing the rule that each recipient must pause for a photo with every gift.

Lauren's presents are opened in stages. Today is the first Christmas her parents will not celebrate together since before she was born. Last year at this time, just before she won Fur, her parents had agreed to open presents together, on the premise that maybe things could still be salvaged. This year, no such pretenses are in play, so Lauren must adapt to the split-personality holiday so familiar to children of divorce. She spent last night with her mom and that side of the family in the house where she grew up. This morning she rose feeling numb, knowing she was obliged to visit her dad in a new apartment she had yet to see. To her surprise, Christmas in this foreign environment actually takes the edge off. Seeing him settled in, being able to picture his things in his new world, lessens the mystery of his new life somewhat. While things are still not effortless, she says, "I feel like I have my dad back. I can see the man who raised me." And yet once the whole thing is over, she finds herself emotionally exhausted.

Kristen's holiday poses a kind of endurance test. At her aunt Bethany's house, three or four dozen people show up for Christmas every year. Everyone gathers in the living room and stakes a spot, with chairs and couches being prime real estate, because otherwise they will be stuck standing or sitting on the floor for three or four hours. The length stems from the inflexible nature of the ritual: There is only one Santa handing out all the gifts, and only one present may be opened at a time, with the gift's giver and recipient named aloud, and all eyes focused on the opening and then the thanks. No second gift may appear on the floor simultaneously, indeed not until the first is completely appreciated; and if the current gift is a children's toy, it gets assembled before the next present may appear. "You try to keep yourself occupied, make sure you have food to eat, while you wait," Kristen explains. "You can leave the room but not for long, and you have to have an excuse. If you have an actual seat, you have to say, 'My spot is saved,' *really loud* and be sure you're heard, or you're shit outta luck."

She's not feeling like standing. She spent a good part of the past week sleeping off migraines in her mom's bed, which is in the darkest room of the house. (Her own room isn't especially inviting these days, as it slowly morphs into storage space.) She's had more blood work done and finally snagged a doctor's appointment, but no relief has yet come, so she's been trapped in a cycle of headaches, lost hours, medicinal relief, bursts of energy, and sleep. Trying to ward off the headache she can just feel coming on, she already took a pre-Bethany's nap today, knowing how much energy the giftathon requires.

One person not at Aunt Bethany's and not on Kristen's gift list is Chance. They broke up after the Cameron Parish trip, with Kristen shouting at him over the phone about how he ought to be treating her, and Chance no match for the human maelstrom that a passionate Kristen can be. Since the breakup, her MySpace and Facebook pages have been flooded with sympathetic notes from her Rhinestone Sisters, which touches her, even as she wonders whether she did the right thing. She ran into Chance last night at a bonfire on the levees—the first time she'd seen him since the breakup—and though it was awkward, it wasn't a horror show either, which makes her wonder whether or not they're really finished. She finds herself walking a fine line between tough girl and softy. "I honestly don't know what's going to happen with us, but whatever happens happens. I have my own life to live."

Chelsea isn't really entertaining any such doubts about Jace, but the same can't be said for him. He keeps calling and still acts territorial. Recently, when she went on a first date with a boy from her class, "It was so annoying. Jace kept calling and whining, upset that I hadn't gone to his holiday party with him." She wants to untangle herself from him entirely, but they somehow end up hanging out from time to time, which she blames on the fact that they stayed together two years. She's only half joking when she says, "I think I'm emotionally damaged from this."

As New Year's Eve approaches, Brandy still has someone to kiss, but she's not sure that's a good thing. Considering that Juicy dotes on her and even spoils her (for instance, buying her a beautiful new suit for D.C. Mardi Gras), Brandy should feel happier than she does. The truth is, she's feeling trapped. "I do love him, but I have no time for what *I* need to do. He wants to be there for *everything*. He's so supportive but he talks about 'our' future, when this all just happened so quickly." She feels ungrateful for not wanting to stick with a boyfriend whose attention many girls would die for, but it's not working for her. "As awful as this sounds, I think I need to focus on *my* goals, not 'ours.' " She knows in her heart she's going to have to break up with him, but the thought scares her, tapping into a completely contradictory emotion. "I am extremely fearful of being alone. I realize I'm only twenty-two, but the thought just terrifies me."

No wonder, then, that New Year's Eve isn't quite the celebration it could be. Her mom cooks dinner and Brandy stays in for the evening, and they drink a good bit together. Juicy, who doesn't know that his future is sealed, stops by for a couple of hours, but the visit is low-key, and he's gone before twelve. When the LaPlace fireworks erupt in the sky at midnight, Brandy doesn't even go outside to watch.

Across town, in a development only surprising if you have

never been young and in love, Kristen spends New Year's Eve with none other than Chance, who has started feeling more comfortable around her family. They have spent the day watching football in her MeMaw and PaPaw's living room, a purple-and-gold shrine to LSU, and are now heading off on a double date to see more levee bonfires. The cool night air and blazing towers serve as the perfect romantic backdrop as Kristen and Chance ring in the New Year once again a couple.

Lauren isn't worrying about romance or parties tonight. She and her boyfriend, Bryant, are an old song at this point, one that has played off and on for four years. Though they'd been broken up during the worst events of the summer, they got back together in the fall, much to Lauren's mother's dismay. Bryant and Lauren's mom are not big fans of each other, which has led to major arguments between mother and daughter lately. Lauren isn't worried, though; she's just happy to have one relationship in her life that isn't complicated right now.

Because of that, she doesn't feel bad about spending New Year's doing homework. "I know, I'm boring!" she says cheerfully. Last year on this night, with her parents' split still fresh, she had been sure that things would get better over time. But things seemed to spiral only downward: her parents' divorce followed by her encounter with the stalker and then her sister's near death. This year, Lauren just can't bring herself to pin too many high hopes on the New Year just yet.

Chelsea never does. "For some reason, all my New Years are horrible, and this one's no exception," she tells me. All day long, Jace has been calling, and all day long she has taken his calls, which means that all day long they have been fighting. He seems to have accepted the breakup but only in that it means now he doesn't have to feel guilty about not doing things she wants to do. Emotionally, however, he keeps laying claim to Chelsea, trying to keep her on the line. "I'm sticking to my guns but he won't make it easy."

As midnight approaches, she tries to dance off the breakup with a crowd at a Lafayette club. But with every minute closer to the tolling of the bells, she feels more and more alone, even surrounded by her friends on the dance floor. In her mind, she keeps replaying Jace's annoying plea just before she left for the club: "Don't kiss anyone at midnight. Please—I mean it!" She should be free of him, but tell that to her heart. Strong enough to leave a guy doesn't mean hard-hearted enough to forget him. When the New Year rings in, the streamers have barely touched the dance floor before she's headed out the door and driving home alone. She will be in bed by twelve-thirty.

By the second week of January, Jace is not alone in his un-wanted status: Juicy has also become an ex-boyfriend, and so has Chance, for the second time in a month. This is a good thing, probably, for the girls are only two weeks from the start of what will be both the high point of their reigns and also the most stressful period. Over the span of a week and a half, they'll spend four days in the nation's capital, immersed in the pageantry of D.C. Mardi Gras, then return home for three days, before traveling to Baton Rouge for the ultimate competition, Queen of Queens. Taken together, from the lavish D.C. ceremony to the tension of head-to-head battle, these ten days are a festival queen's Olympics.

With no boyfriend, her spring classes still weeks off, and having quit her Buckle job, Chelsea finds that planning for the one-two punch of the big events gives her something to focus on. "It seems the closer they are, the more they become my life." For D.C. Mardi Gras, she'll be wearing Brooke's old Frog gown, a dark green silk sheath, and she has two potential competition gowns, both blue, to choose from for Queen of Queens. The more conservative is an elegantly ruched-and-beaded number with a train, a dress perfect for illustrating a fairy tale; the other dress is more Miami Beach than Baton Rouge, a billowy blue number that looks like gold paint has been splattered across it. The latter has more distinct personality (her mom thinks it says Chelsea all over), but Brooke warns her that Queen of Queens is simply not a squeaky-wheel setting—the judges don't typically reward the girls who defy convention. Chelsea makes the safer choice and returns the risky option.

Tiny as she is, her dress needs dramatic alterations before it will fit. "Let me tell you, to take an eight to a double zero is not easy!" And that is only half of it. The reduced silhouette of the gown will emphasize her scoliosis, making it clear how much higher one hip is than the other, so the dressmaker has ordered a prosthetic hip for her to wear inside her panty hose. She's never heard of such a thing, but she's glad for the help: She just wants to feel beautiful for her coming moment in the sun.

"I am so excited about the whole experience!" she tells

me. "Now that I can see the light at the end, I am running for it as fast as my short, skinny, uneven legs will take me. I really am not nervous about anything, even walking in all my heavy stuff. The worst that can happen is I just take out a couple chairs and a man!"

If only that were true.

13

Bring Your Crown

From the Voy Boards

Good Topic to Discuss: If you are a queen and are arrested during your year should that mean your title should be taken away too?
—*Saw it on the other board*

It is Thursday night in Lafayette, and as it does in most cities, the weekend begins early for the young. Downtown becomes a stream of girls in tops that cling like liquid skin, and burly guys in untucked shirts with more flair than the ones they wear to work or class. Chelsea and seven of her friends are tucked into a banquette table at Bonsai Sushi to celebrate a twenty-first birthday. The octet barely fits around the table, but it's the perfect-size group for a celebration—not so big that its splits into separate camps, not so small that the birthday girl will feel underappreciated. Peer at them from across the room and they seem the picture of youth: harmless, happy, exuberant.

For Chelsea, the meal is an antidote to dealing with Jace, proverbial bad penny that he is. For all the inattentiveness that plagued their relationship, he dogs her steps now. Just this afternoon, he called again and made her feel bad about not loving him, despite their having been broken up for two months already. His method as usual was indirect, cracking jokes rather than overtly criticizing her. No matter, by the time they were off the phone, he had scored again, convincing her that she's the villain. Tonight a birthday party—with people who don't make her feel awful—is just the remedy she needs. She orders her favorite dish, crunchy rolls of shrimp and mango, and settles in. Actually, her order is not plural: Her entire dinner is *one* crunchy roll, cut into several small pieces perfectly sized for picking at while nursing sodas and talking with her friends. At ninety-five pounds, she's never been a big eater, and with Jace stressing her out, she really has no appetite at all.

> *The queen of any festival should not be involved in any criminal activities. If she is arrested during her reign then she should be stripped of her title. Of course it's all in who you are with this incident. Let's see what they will do about it. She should never have won that title in the first place.* —*Wondering*

The friends close the place down, which isn't hard: Bonsai's sushi chefs put down their knives at ten P.M. Luckily, eighty-year-old City Bar, a local institution that is one of her friends' favorite haunts, is just a stone's throw away. City Bar is packed on Thursdays, when girls get their drinks free after midnight, but Chelsea doesn't hold out that long: She's usually a one-drink girl on nights like this, and she isn't going to wait an hour and a half for it. She orders something fun, a Long Island Iced Tea. It's only six ounces, half the size of a beer, so she can tell herself that while drinking at twenty is a crime, it's literally a small crime. Looking around the dark space, lit by a glowing bar top and the constant motion of a half dozen TV screens overheard, she can see plenty of wasted people and feel smug: She's not one of *them*. She takes her first sip.

This is it, the moment she'll look back on with regret and embarrassment and shame, the moment that starts a chain of events she can't undo. In her heart, Chelsea knows a Long Island is a strong drink, but she doesn't know *how* strong. If she was a bartender, she'd realize that a Long Island is one of the most dangerous cocktails available because of its comparatively high alcohol content. It contains five kinds of liquor, their combined body-slamming punch initially masked by the sweetness of sugar syrup and the tang of sour mix. Plus, the drink completely lacks ameliorating ingredients like the seltzer in a mojito or the juice in a piña colada. For someone her size, this might as well be two drinks, three even, the toxic equivalent of half a six-pack. Having consumed only a few ounces of shrimp, rice, seaweed, and mango to absorb the blow, she is *thisclose* to taking the drink's full blast on an empty stomach. She sips slowly, talking to her friends over the din, and like always, when she finishes the Long Island, she switches over to water and soda for the rest of the night, sure that this will dilute the effects of the cocktail.

> *Who was arrested????   —No name*
>
> *Name and title?   —Wondering*
>
> *The Miss Frog Queen was arrested for DWI and Speeding.   —No name*
>
> *OMG . . . FROG queen lmao!!!*
>> *—Who would want that title*
>
> *It is a VERY distinguished title . . . until now I guess   —No name*

It's after midnight and the night is still young, but one of Chelsea's friends needs to leave and she realizes she's left her purse in Chelsea's car. While the party at City Bar throbs on, Chelsea walks the friend to her Mustang and then they hug good night. Though the rest of her crowd is still at City Bar, thinking she'll return, she doesn't feel like crossing the shadowy blocks back to the bar alone. She decides to call it an early night.

Driving away from the city, away from her friends, she cruises toward Rayne, just twenty minutes away. The thickly settled city areas disappear behind her as she navigates the dark back roads home. All alone in her car, she can hear Jace's mocking, wheedling voice in her head, and she starts to cry.

How can he possibly still make her feel like this? She blinks at the tears, keeps her eyes on the road, nervously noting the Lafayette sheriff's car, which has just pulled alongside her and then cruised on by.

She just wants to be home, safe in bed, crying herself to sleep. The closer to Rayne, the faster she drives. The road already has a fifty-five limit, so it's hardly a sleepy country lane, and it's an old habit to speed here. In the back of her head, a voice should be warning her—*You already passed a cop*—but she races along, frustration and fatigue steering her on. And then she sees him: The sheriff has turned around, almost as if he's waiting just for her. Which he is.

He turns on his lights. Chelsea pulls over, thinking, *I smell like a bar. I have a stamp on my hand. This does not look good.* She knows where this is going.

> *WTG Chelsea Richard, Miss Frog Festival*
> *Queen on your OWI and speeding charge!*
> *—I'm so glad my daughter looks up to you!*
> *You are truly a piece of work!*
>
> *Wow. This is a terrible board. I'm sad I stumbled across this.   —No name*

The officer is older, but he's not grandfatherly; he has a look on his face that says, *Gotcha!* In the voice of a man who enjoys his job, he asks if she knew she was speeding. "Yes, sir," she says.

He writes this down. She doesn't know what to do next

and blurts out, "If I wasn't speeding when you passed me the first time, why'd you turn around and come back?"

There's just a hint of a gleam in his eye. "Oh, I knew you'd speed *eventually*."

All of this is prelude, of course, for him to deliver the big-money question. "Have you had anything to drink?"

Chelsea decides that the truth is on her side—she ate, had a single cocktail, drank water, and waited two hours—and she doesn't hesitate. "Yes, sir. One drink earlier."

"What did you have?"

"A Long Island."

The sheriff is almost smiling. "That's one of the more *potent* drinks, you know."

Using a standard blood alcohol calculator, a ninety-five-pound female who consumes a six-ounce Long Island would have roughly a .12 blood alcohol content (BAC) if tested an hour and a half after drinking, and a .9 BAC after two hours, still just exceeding the level of legal intoxication. It is approaching three hours since Chelsea's drink, so it is possible—but not very likely—that her BAC has dropped to within legal limits. Only one of the two people in this conversation understands the odds against her.

When the trooper says, "Step out of the vehicle," five words that motorists never forget, it begins to sink in for Chelsea that the night is going to be longer than she had imagined. Any long-ago buzz from the drink has dissipated in the cold-water shock of being pulled over, and it's hard to believe he's making her do the field sobriety test. She touches her finger to her nose. She walks a straight line, forward and back. It is humiliating, or would be if anyone could see her, but she feels vindicated that she isn't a mess, that she can complete both tasks with ease. Still, that's not enough: Yes, she can *do* everything, but the sheriff reminds her that a Long Island is a mighty strong drink, so he's not convinced.

Chelsea starts shaking. There is no way to protest, no way to stop this. He's police and she's a girl who just admitted to drinking and driving. They are all alone out here, two figures in a tiny drama playing out beneath a vast black sky, a set of flashing lights the only illumination for as far as the eye can see in either direction. The sheriff knows who holds the power. He produces a Breathalyzer and says, "I'm going to make you breathe into this for me."

She knows that the BAC limit for someone under twenty-one is an unforgiving .02 and that she will fail this. But then she sees the silver lining: There's no way she's over .08, the legal limit for adults, so taking the Breathalyzer will give her a chance to salvage things. She's thinking that this will be a way for her to prove she wasn't sloppy drunk, that when everyone finds out, at least this will show she wasn't wasted.

Except that she blows .085. Chelsea Richard, the 2008 Miss Rayne Frog Festival Queen, is legally drunk.

All the things she thought she did "right" have conspired against her. What she called eating barely provided food to mute the effect of the alcohol. All the soda sped up the emptying of her stomach, making her body absorb the alcohol faster and harder. And, of course, she chose just about the worst possible "one drink." The road to her personal hell was well-paved with intentions that don't interest the sheriff; all that matters at this dark hour is that she did two things she knows in her heart are wrong: She drank underage and then got behind the wheel. With a righteous gleam in his eye, the sheriff handcuffs her.

Good Point: is she even 21 yet?   —*Wonderful*

No she is not 21 so even by just having one drink it was still ILLEGAL   —*No name*

Now that is sad   —*No name*

At the police station in Lafayette, things are slow, not a lot of activity this particular night, so the officers on duty can focus on Chelsea. They're a jovial lot, laughing and making jokes the whole time she gets fingerprinted and then stands, eyes full of tears, for her mug shot. And when she starts to cry, serious sobs as the reality of the situation finally hits her, the men stop joking around and try to make her feel better. "We're not making fun of you," one of them tells her, and the others agree. No, they assure her, they're laughing at the sheriff who brought her in—they call him Barney Fife and mock him for handcuffing her and dragging her down here.

But her tears aren't for the cops at all and she says so. "I'm not worried about what you think. I'm worried about my community. When this gets out, it's going to be so much bigger."

It is seven A.M. when they let her leave with her mom. The sun is up and it shows the tiredness on Vicki Richard's face. She's not a talker, so she doesn't say too much, and what she does say walks a fine line between being upset that Chelsea has gotten herself into this situation and being relieved that her daughter isn't dead, which is another phone call she could have received after this sequence of events. She had never gotten so much as a note home from school about Chelsea, so it seems unreal that the first call she gets is from a police station. And she will have to weather this particular parental crisis alone, as Chelsea's dad is offshore, on an oil rig, and will be for three more days. She turns to Chelsea in the car, her daughter barely able to look up. "Okay," she says, "what happens next?"

The Miss Frog Queen was arrested for DWI and Speeding. It was listed in the Advertiser for all to see. Word has it she is NOT being stripped . . . doesn't seem fair to me   —No name

Wow, people really like to talk about others getting arrested for DUI on this board. How do yall know that it is her, could be the same name but different person . . . Yall need to make sure that it is her not just someone with the same name. Yall don't want to post something that isn't true!!!   —No name

It was in the Daily Advertiser, WITH her name
and address . . . its her   —No name

Chelsea is in her room, the lights off, trying to will herself
to sleep at nine A.M., when the phone rings. It's Brooke and
her tone is bright, breezy.

"What's up, Chelsea?"

"Nothing." *Does she know?*

"Anything you want to tell me?"

Chelsea dies inside and can't say the truth, but even her lie
comes out as a question. "No?"

"Chelsea, I'm not playing." The breeze, the artifice, is
gone.

Tears flow. "You know! You know already!"

"*Everyone* knows. It was in the *Advertiser.*" Brooke feels
everything you'd expect: hurt, furious, shocked, betrayed. But
for the time being she focuses on the girl on the other end of
the line and what that girl's actions will mean for the town.
Brooke thinks Chelsea needs to start making amends immediately, first and foremost with Angie, the Chamber of Commerce president who is the Frog Queen's official boss. "Now,
you get on that phone before it gets any worse."

Cajuns must love arrest reports—and love 'em fresh—
because the overnight arrests are already posted on the Web
site of the *Daily Advertiser* newspaper, complete with vital statistics and offense. For pure schadenfreude, once you've seen
the report in the paper, you can visit the sheriff's office Web
site to see the mug shot online, as long as you snoop quickly.

(Records are removed after forty-eight hours.) Chelsea's arrest is not yet ten hours old and already she's news.

Ms. Cheryl's mother saw it first, calling Cheryl to warn her, and Cheryl made a warning call of her own to Angie. Angie made the call to Brooke, knowing how this news would wound someone whose sister was killed by a drunk driver. Better she hears it from a friend.

When Chelsea finally works up her courage to call Angie, she learns that an emergency meeting of the Chamber of Commerce has been scheduled for that afternoon. She can only imagine how widely the story will have traveled by then.

> *What about most festival's contracts stating that*
> *"their queen must behave in a manner becoming*
> *of a lady at all times during her reign"?*
> —*This behavior is definitely not very "becoming" at all*
>
> *She is a "piece of work." Drinking and driving,*
> *etc. . . .*
> —*Not something my daughter should be looking up to*
>
> *I hope that you encourage your daughter to look*
> *elsewhere for a role model then.*
> —*If this is the way you feel about her*

By noon, people have started digging for dirt. Several residents call the Rayne police to find out what charges have been filed, a fact that the chief passes on to Ms. Cheryl, who is glad at least that the busybodies have called the wrong station. (Chelsea was booked in Lafayette, not Rayne.) If this snowballs, Ms. Cheryl's just not sure the chamber can protect Chelsea. And, to be honest, she's not sure they should. "I could just shake her. She thinks this has happened to her, you know. But what happens to her happens to the town, to the festival. If she takes a hit, she's gonna take the chamber with her. I love that girl, and I mean it, but this was as stupid as it gets." Her voice is a thick stew of pain and anger. "We're dumbstruck—nobody knows what's going to happen."

At first nothing happens. Jan, the secretary of the chamber, is there when Chelsea and Vicki arrive, and she is encouraging. The newest members of the board, Pesh and Nicky, both barely in their thirties, are close enough to Chelsea's age that they can remember what it's like to be that young, and perhaps that is why neither of them goes too hard on her. But Ms. Cheryl, whose pageant crowned Chelsea, and Angie, whose chamber holds her contract, are rightly pissed that she could be so foolish.

They ask her what she's thinking, what she wants to do, what she can possibly make from this mess, but the questions come too soon: Chelsea still hardly believes it has happened. She hasn't had time to let it sink in, much less explain it to others. So she just keeps repeating that it was only one drink and she's sorry but she thought she was okay and she's sorry and—it's a loop that she can't yet improve on, and it isn't winning her much sympathy. She thinks that repeating how the officers called the sheriff "Barney Fife" will prove to the chamber that she was the victim of wrong place, wrong cop, but this only convinces them that she doesn't understand the gravity of her actions. The good news for her is that the chamber decides not to do anything rash. Angie tells her, "We're not gonna take your crown yet. Let's just let the weekend pass and see what happens."

Chelsea keeps saying, "Okay, okay, thank you, thank you," to the board, grateful for their understanding and relieved that it isn't all over for her just yet. Even though she feels physically ill, she clings to the belief that the board is still behind her. But her comfort is premised on the gentlest possible reading of what they're saying. She isn't hearing the complete message: "Lie low for now, but Monday may be a different story."

Whatever the outcome, Cheryl will not be around to see it—she's about to leave on a cruise to the Caribbean with Miles. January is as close to downtime as she ever gets—no pageants, no fund-raisers, no holidays, and no RV rallies. Though she's pretty much the best person at crisis management in town, and the one most able to talk straight with Chelsea, she's going to be drinking Bahama Mamas on a boat somewhere while the drama plays out.

It isn't a good weekend for anyone. Chelsea doesn't call her friends, and she doesn't even think about going out; she hides in her room, crying on and off, not eating. Her brother, Scott, learns from a friend that one of the girls his sister had beaten in a past Rayne pageant has posted Chelsea's mug shot on her MySpace page. He tells Vicki, saying he wants her to keep the news from his sister, but his mom thinks a family plan to deceive Chelsea would only make her feel worse when she discovers the story later, as she surely would.

The MySpace girl isn't the only one of Chelsea's former competitors who knows something's up. Without explaining the specific circumstances, Angie has been calling Jennifer, Chelsea's first runner-up, to have her prepare for the possibility of replacing Chelsea, not just in Rayne but in D.C. and at Queen of Queens, tantalizing prospects for any girl.

Angie feels that she has no other choice but to make these calls. D.C. Mardi Gras is not an event that a town or festival can simply skip; it's a private event, so organizers may invite whom they choose. The fear is that if a queen doesn't show after confirming that she will be there, her festival might well be dropped from the rotation, and it could then take years or decades to make the cut again. Being part of D.C. Mardi Gras lends credibility to a festival and it is a major attraction for contestants, so *someone* from Rayne has to go—but Angie is beginning to doubt that it will be Chelsea.

Angie feels the heat as the word spreads. Online, it's not just the Tabloids board discussing the story; even the Positive board is ripe with opinions about the situation, many posters already holding Angie and Cheryl to the flame for their perceived inaction. In the nonvirtual world, people have been calling the newspapers, and the newspapers have called Angie. Word on the grapevine is that the aunt of a runner-up has written a letter to the editor condemning the town's inaction.

A local TV station has been calling around to find out if it's true that the Frog Queen was arrested. Angie's pretty tired of picking up the phone to hear yet another person tell her that if the chamber lets Chelsea keep her crown, it will make the town look bad.

"I'm pretty open-minded compared to some directors," she tells me, her voice tired and husky with fatigue. "And I know she's been through a lot. But she just doesn't seem to get it—calling up Brooke, after all she's been through, and saying she wasn't sloppy drunk, like that's the point. She doesn't realize that she's taking all of us with her." Angie doesn't think there's any chance Chelsea will offer to step down to spare the town. "My life couldn't be so easy."

Chelsea knows what she is expected to do, but something in her resists. "Nothing like this has ever happened to me. I guess the thing that really, really kills me is that for so long, for my entire life, I've done a lot of really great things, good things, and I've never remotely made a mistake like this. The day I did, the first mistake I make, the idea that it's all over . . ." She trails off and her voice closes up, the sound of a girl who's been crying a lot trying not to cry again. "I worked so hard to be Frog Queen—it doesn't make sense to just walk away now."

> this is jmho, but if I was the queen that this
> happened to, and my crown was not taken, first
> to save face for everyone I would give it back and
> let the first place winner take the crown   —jmho

I'm sure she is humiliated. Very sad turn of
events. Personally, I'd give up my title . . .
        —*No name*

She should be stripped no question asked.
        —*Charges dropped or not!*

But the charges have been dropped. And look at
the Rayne Police Chief being arrested and
charged with DWI.
        —*Look in your own back yard, Those who*
        live in glass houses . . .

The fact of the matter is that when you are a
queen . . . Queens are held to a higher stan-
dard. You should be more careful of what you do.
EVERY little girl looks up to you!   —*No name*

Even though she knew the call might come, Chelsea is
still upset on Monday when Angie rings to say that she's already talked to Jennifer about D.C. and Queen of Queens.
"Can you help Jen, tell her what she needs to know to get
ready?" Chelsea is noncommittal, her mind racing at this almost casual question, the first undeniable indication to her of
what the chamber wants. Angie isn't being callous here; she's
simply doing her job to watch out for the chamber and the
festival. But still it stings when she says, "Come by the chamber with all your stuff. Bring your crown and banner."

The simplest thing for Chelsea to do at this point is to

agree, then hang up the phone and cry. For a shy girl, one not used to bucking authority, this would be the predictable response. But she's a queen now, and this isn't what she does. "Give me till the afternoon," she tells Angie. "And can you fax me a copy of the contract? I just want someone to go over it for me."

Angie seems unfazed, as far as Chelsea can tell by her voice. "Sure, sure . . ."

But then an hour passes and a second hour, and no contract. Chelsea does something she's only done once since the arrest: She leaves her house and heads into town. At the chamber's office, she is relieved to find that Angie is nowhere in sight. Jan, apologizing that the fax is on the fritz, gives Chelsea a hard copy of the contract. Chelsea can hardly wait to get in her car and drive away before anyone sees—or, worse, confronts—her.

After a call to a contract lawyer she picked from the phone book, things look up for her for the first time in days. He tells her the document is full of holes. His opinion is that the agreement can't bear close scrutiny.

Chelsea calls Angie to say that she is ready for their meeting after all, but that instead of a crown and banner, what she'll be bringing is her contract and opinion as to its validity. Depending on whose side you are on, this is either pure selfishness or a model of self-determination. One thing all parties would agree on is this: Saying no to the Chamber of Commerce is the ballsiest thing Chelsea has ever done in her life.

Now it's Angie's turn to put things off. She is already dealing with a son who is home ill today, and the last thing

she needs is to have this fight with a twenty-year-old, especially if the specter of a legal dispute is in the air. She puts the
meeting off for a day, time in which both she and Pesh meet
with the chamber's lawyer. Like Chelsea's attorney, the chamber's counsel reaches the conclusion that the contract won't
hold up. Short of Chelsea being convicted of a felony, the
chamber can't fire her easily; a first DUI (variously called a
DWI and OWI on the Voy boards) is a misdemeanor and, besides, she hasn't been convicted of *anything*. Moreover, she
won't be: Louisiana law allows that a first-offense charge can,
with the District Attorney's approval, be dropped from your
record if you complete community service and do not re-
offend. The chamber would lose this battle in any court—and
still have the same Frog Queen after spending money to publicly try to oust her. It just isn't worth it.

When Angie and Chelsea finally do talk, it is tense. Angie
announces that the chamber has decided not to fight to take
the crown. Chelsea realizes that she should consider this a gift,
that she should be grateful, but she also knows that it was her
refusal to back down that has pushed them into this corner.
She tries to explain her rationale: "I've already made a shitty
example and I can't turn it around if I just walk away." This
is not persuasive to Angie, who still doesn't hear what she
wants to hear: a truly heartfelt apology that doesn't include
an excuse.

The town now must work with a girl it has told to take a
hike. The chamber and the festival board can't ignore how
thoroughly their reputations are entwined with that of their

festival queen: It isn't just rhetoric to say that the queen represents the town, her conduct a cultural barometer for its val-
ues. No matter how much they love Chelsea as a person, all
the Rayne officials know they will now be judged for what
happens (or doesn't happen) next. All the people in other
communities jealous of the festival's popularity and prominence, all the people who have a gripe with the chamber, all
the people who have a bone to pick with Ms. Cheryl's pageants, and everyone looking for corruption or shady back-
room deals in local politics—fair or not, this gives them fresh
ammunition. The chamber's frustration and anxiety are unavoidable.

But there is also something impressive about Chelsea not
quickly folding under the stress of this situation. No one expected there to be a will of steel beneath the makeup and
size-zero gowns. But what is the festival queen tradition if not
proof of girl power? Anyone whose average week includes
working, going to class, traveling across the state, and then, say,
riding a bull on demand, isn't likely to be a frail flower. This is
especially true in Rayne, where the Frog Queen's obvious
female role models include Angie and Ms. Cheryl. In a way,
despite being in conflict with them, Chelsea is emulating
the strength and fierce determination of both women, and
proving her festival queen mettle to boot.

Still, as she later describes to me how it will feel to wear
the crown after her town has made it clear it doesn't want her
to, notes of doubt mingle with the bravado in her voice. "I
know," she sighs. "It would be easier just to let 'em take it and

walk away. But you can't really judge a person on how she acts when things are easy. You find out what she's like when it's hard." When I remind her that she's going to have plenty of opportunity to test this theory, she starts to laugh, but the sound catches in her throat. She stays quiet for a long time.

why was the charges dropped?   —*No name*

that is how they do business
   —*because she is a rayne girl . . . above the law*

If they wanted me to keep the title I would not go to q of q's [Queen of Queens] and know that everyone is talking about it, i would just be to- tally ashamed   —*jmho*

Who cares about q of qs. She is going to d.c. too
      —*No name*

they should really give the title to the first run- ner up and let her go to D.C. . . . its almost like they are giving her a slap on the wrist and saying OH its okay! Go on and get arrested. You can keep your title and still reap all the benefits   —*No name*

Angie knows that the old contract doesn't allow for Chelsea to be stripped of her title, but she decides to do something that will let the people of Rayne know that the problem has not gone unnoticed. She asks the chamber lawyer to craft a new contract, one that is more explicit both in what is expected of a queen and how she may be ousted. This will cover the chamber legally should any new problems arise, while also providing Angie with a response to critics who say no one is minding the shop when it comes to the queen's behavior. She asks Chelsea to sign this additional agreement and to abide by it for the remainder of her reign.

Chelsea already has a contract and, if she wishes, she can make the chamber live with the original deal. But she knows that agreeing to this second contract will be a show of good faith. When Angie calls a special meeting to unveil the new document, Chelsea arrives at the chamber perfectly willing to sign, to do anything it takes to start earning back their trust.

Today is Ms. Cheryl's first day at work since returning from the cruise and learning that her Frog Queen has refused the chamber's request to step down. Ms. Cheryl's so mad at Chelsea, she can hardly look at her. Angie produces the new contract without fanfare. Chelsea tries to breach the gap between herself and all of them. "I'm not here to make your life miserable or to cause trouble," she tells them. "I'm just standing up for myself with as much dignity and respect as I can." Angie knows that nothing requires Chelsea to play along here, and so thanks her for signing, but that is all the goodwill Angie can muster.

Before Chelsea can leave, Ms. Cheryl wants a word with her. With the others gone, it is just the two of them in Ms. Cheryl's office, sitting on either side of a desk but divided by more than simple wood. Ms. Cheryl tells Chelsea that it's not just Rayne that has had to draw up new contracts—all over the state, festivals are hurriedly rewriting their agreements to be more ironclad and strict. "That costs time and money they don't have because of you." This accusation strikes Chelsea as unfair—how can she be blamed for the weak wording of contracts used since before she was born? Wisely, she doesn't say this. Ms. Cheryl is only getting started.

"Every time you defend yourself and say, 'I only had one drink,' that's not an apology, that's an excuse."

"But I say 'one drink' because that's all it took."

"Well, you know what? All people hear is the excuse. People don't think you're sorry, Chelsea. They think you're sorry you *got caught*."

Chelsea's cheeks have been burning but now her eyes start to sting. Something in this attack hurts more than the rest of it. She knows that people think ill of her because of the arrest and some say she should give up her crown. But it's more wounding, a deep jab at her true character, if people really think she's so callous that she's not even sorry to have caused this much grief. Ms. Cheryl plows on.

"People who have had to suffer the consequences of drunk driving before, they say you got away with it. And people who believe the spoiled-beauty-queen idea, they think you prove them right, because you got off so easy."

The handcuffs, the newspaper, the humiliating MySpace page, the hours of sobbing into her pillow, the five pounds she has lost in as many days—it doesn't feel easy to Chelsea. But it is up to Ms. Cheryl, more than anyone, to drive home the message that no one is going to cry for a girl who drinks and drives and lives to tell.

Because Chelsea has always known she could get a straight answer from Ms. Cheryl, she asks the question she hasn't dared ask anyone else involved: "Do you think I should have stepped down?"

Ms. Cheryl doesn't even pause: "Yes." Still, she didn't get where she is by lingering over hypotheticals. She's a master of working with the real, so she lets this opinion linger on heavy air for only a moment before adding, "But now you've made your decision, so the real question is, 'What do we do about it?'"

"What do you want me to do?"

"You have *got* to stop explaining. Nobody cares. You gotta sit in your house and practice just saying, 'I was wrong and I'm sorry.'"

Chelsea opens her mouth, but Ms. Cheryl cuts her off. She isn't playing. *"End of sentence."* As someone who has been in the public eye for two decades, Ms. Cheryl understands that if there is any chance of this blowing over, Chelsea will have to learn to swallow not just her pride but all the words that come with it. "Practice it at home. 'I was wrong and I'm sorry.' *Period.*"

> *I think she is getting her fair share of public hu-*
> *miliation. I don't think anyone has the right to*
> *judge her unless you can look her in the eye and*
> *tell her NEVER IN YOUR LIFE have you*

*had ONE drink and then drove home. Come on
people, don't tell me you NEVER got behind
the wheel after ONE drink. I agree that she
should not have done it, but EVERYONE
makes mistakes.*

> *—She was just unlucky and got caught*

It's not about humiliation, she broke the law.

> *—She should give up the title*

Amen   —No name

*I will never say I myself have never had 1 drink
and then drove because I have. I know last year
at a function, they were serving wine and several
mothers of contestants were drinking and then as
I was leaving they got into their vehicles and
left. I myself was guilty of that that night and
the same ones who were there that night are
probably the ones on here making comments
about it!!!   —No name*

Word spreads more slowly now; some days it feels as if the story might die down, and then others there's new wind lifting the gossip sails. Chelsea hasn't told most of her friends, hoping those who missed the news in the paper will keep missing it, and when they call to see if she wants to go out, she ducks their offers, making lame excuses or none at all. One person she does contact herself is the Ms. Frog Queen, the Rayne royalty who lives farthest away. Chelsea thinks her fellow queen shouldn't have to hear the story late and third-hand, so she sends a note to explain what happened. She gets a terse reply: "Thank you for letting me know." It's the last she will ever hear from the Ms. Queen.

Every few days, it seems, a new round of attacks flashes across the Voy boards. Chelsea doesn't read them herself: Brooke does, and then she passes the gist of it on during their conversations. Chelsea calls almost every day, and Brooke tries her best to be supportive, but the truth is that the task is weighing heavily on her. In a classic proof of the ironic maxim that no good deed goes unpunished, the whole thing has reawakened the trauma of losing her sister, a tragedy that created an awful void that can't be filled. Tamping down her own pain, Brooke soldiers on; never the kind of person who would abandon someone in crisis, she digs deep to help steer Chelsea through the thicket ahead. She has no intention of sugarcoating things, however. Brooke thinks there's no way to avoid all of the Rhinestone Sisters hearing the whole story, and knows some of them will not be so kind. She warns Chelsea sternly, "It's coming your way."

When Chelsea shows up at the ribbon-cutting for a new gift shop, her first formal duty since she re-signed her contract, the chamber officers all act friendly enough, if not exactly warm. The townspeople she meets greet her neutrally, though who knows what they'll say when she's out of earshot. Only Mayor Jimbo reaches out to her directly, addressing the unspoken, and in so doing gives her the first hint that she can survive this.

"You doing okay?" Jimbo asks, offering her a hug. He looks her in the eye, just as she had told him to do in the on-stage interview at her pageant, which now feels like a lifetime ago. "It's gonna be a long road, you know, but don't you hide. Okay?"

When your orders come from the mayor, there's no arguing. She straightens up. "Yes, sir."

14

Like Stars

The fortunate festival queens who hold one of the highly coveted D.C. Ball invitations from the Mystick Krewe of Louisianians know that their Mardi Gras experience won't be remotely ordinary. For one thing, it's starting a month before Fat Tuesday, when everyone else celebrates; for another, the ball takes place a thousand miles from home in the nation's capital. D.C. Mardi Gras doesn't pretend to be the real thing—it's the souped-up, tricked-out version, the Maserati of parties.

The luxe treatment starts on the last Wednesday of January. Traditionally, before the queens leave Louisiana on a private jet, they enjoy a breakfast meeting with the governor at his mansion. It's supposed to be a kick-off event that demonstrates the importance of the girls' roles in Louisiana cultural life, and this year it comes with the bonus that Governor Bobby Jindal is being touted as a Republican rising star. As the GOP is the party of almost all the queens here, the national buzz around Jindal adds an extra frisson of thrill to what already promises to be an exciting first event. And it would be—if the governor would show up.

Considering that this is an 8:30 A.M. meeting, it wouldn't seem like other appointments could keep him at bay, but the girls arrive and then wait, and then wait, and then wait for their audience. There is no room set aside for their visit, so twenty-five girls wait in the mansion's foyer with only one couch available for sitting. Most the them mill about chatting, eyes on the time. Brandy is dead tired—she'd rather be sleeping than standing—and Lauren is anxious, not about this meeting but about the prospect of a four-day trip with her mother, with whom things have been tense lately. Chelsea is guarded, this being her first time in the presence of other queens since her arrest, and it would be much easier to get through the morning if the governor were there to provide a distraction. Kristen is wired, excited at being in the governor's mansion, loving all the Mardi Gras masks and beads woven through the Christmas decorations. Even so, she's ready to roll and, diehard GOP girl or not, she finds it annoying that they must all sit here cooling their high heels.

When Governor Jindal and his wife finally arrive a half hour late, he is pleasant but awkward, and he seems confused as to why they are there. "Now, how many of you are going to Washington?" he asks, an innocent enough question, except that the whole point of their visit is that *all* of them have been selected to go and he's supposed to be congratulating them. Lauren's thinking, *Mister—you can't even fake like you know?* Chelsea doesn't like anything about him, from the way he speaks to the way he carries himself. Still, he's the governor and a potential future commander in chief, so the girls take pictures with him quickly, before hurrying out to the bus that will take them to the airport.

The governor's lassitude has made the queens late for their flight, which will now have to depart well behind schedule. Chelsea dreads having to fill more empty time with her fellow queens. She looks around the airport, at girls buying bottles of water or posing for pictures, and wonders, *Does* she *know? Does* she? No one is saying anything if they do, but when Crawfish comes up, Chelsea braces for the worst, only to have the conversation take a surprise direction.

"Hey girl, I know your ex!"

Jace being Chelsea's second-least-favorite topic, she can't think of anything else to say but "Super." Turns out that Crawfish hangs out with one of Jace's best friends and knows all kinds of stories about him. Chelsea can't believe it. "It's like no matter where I go, he is always around!" But Crawfish has no ax to grind on the topic of the breakup, says nothing about the arrest, and is warm and welcoming, for which Chelsea is immediately grateful. It's the beginning of a new friendship.

When the girls finally board the plane, there is a crown kerfuffle. The girls don't like to part with their crown boxes—considering their contents cost thousands of dollars and must be returned, this is not shocking—so many queens have brought them aboard as carry-ons. But the crew wants to put all the boxes in the hold beneath for safety. This also is logical, seeing as how some of the boxes are heavy wooden cubes that you wouldn't want flying at your head in a moment of turbulence. Some of the girls politely refuse, anyway. Kristen is one of them, and she strikes a deal: They can put her box in the hold, but the crown stays on her lap, which itself becomes awkward and uncomfortable over the course of the two-and-a-half-hour flight. (And perhaps not 100 percent safer—you could take an eye out with that thing.)

After they arrive in the snow-covered capital, the rest of the day is reserved for unpacking and sleeping at the Washington Hilton, the hotel perhaps best known for being the site where John Hinckley shot President Reagan. The mammoth curved building reserves all one thousand of its rooms that weekend for Louisianians, and it is usually booked to about 90 percent capacity months before Mardi Gras. In the final days before the event kicks off, the hotel releases the few unclaimed rooms. The unsuspecting guests who have ended up booking these accommodations now seem dazed by the ongoing party around them: throngs of people drinking in the middle of the afternoon, wearing Mardi Gras beads even though it's only January, calling out greetings left and right as if they know everyone else in the building. A large professionally made sign has been hoisted to rename the hotel bar THE 65TH PARISH OF LOUISIANA and, on every floor, when the elevator doors open, Cajun music leads to suites hosting parties for the original sixty-four.

There is little for the queens to do tonight except socialize, talk to representatives from their parishes, and obey the rules set by the Mystick Krewe. The rules boil down to this:

They may only leave the building with permission, must be in their rooms by ten P.M., and may never under any circumstances have a man in their room, even a relative. These safeguards on their virtue are meant to protect the well-being of a group largely composed of small-town girls without urban experience. But the rules also cover the ball, shielding it from responsibility for any harm that might come to the girls (or to their chastity). The ball simply means too much to risk letting any "girls gone wild" behavior tarnish it. For some of the girls—the youngest is seventeen—that seems like a no-brainer, but with a number of college students over twenty-one in the mix, there are always a few who feel a little constrained.

Their behavior here will have two tangible side effects. In the long run, a queen who blows off her duties or conducts herself in disreputable fashion might get her festival uninvited for years to come (and trust me, that is *not* something you would want to have on your shoulders in Louisiana). In the short run, it can also affect a girl's experience at Queen of Queens next week. Because festival queens are only one component of the vast Mardi Gras operation, their reputations aren't going to be a big source of discussion among the rest of the partygoers here, who have to deal with little things like voting in Congress or running utilities. But Queen of Queens will be part of the LAFF convention, an event by and for only festival people at all levels, so any screw-up here will be much discussed there—both for the girls as contestants and for festivals as their employers. According to Ms. Cheryl, the Voy board goes completely berserk every day closer to Queen of Queens, so Mardi Gras gossip is unavoidable.

Most of the girls are here with their parents or representatives from their festivals, which might make it harder to bend the rules, but the girls actually bunk with other queens on a separate floor, which allows more room for play. The Mystick Krewe provides its own official chaperones, who check the girls into their rooms at night, help with any issues that might arise, and make sure they show up for all the required events. The chaperones, Lauren explains, are typically young family members of the event's founders. But here's the rub: The majority of these chaperones are men. Not just men, but twenty-somethings, the kind of strapping, pumped-up lookers that a pulp novel would call "young bucks." It doesn't matter that some of them are married (a few wives also serve as chaperones); it still looks as though someone at central casting keyed in "stud" instead of "chaperone." Some of them, according to the girls, act like it, too.

Chelsea, keenly aware of propriety, can't quite believe these are the people enforcing the moral rectitude of the queens. "The whole chaperone thing creeps me out. They look each girl up and down, like they're trying to see which one of us is the dumbest." While that can't be said of most of the chaperones, it only takes a couple of guys acting inappropriately to cast a tawdry light over the whole group. And the same is true for the queens. If even one girl flirts back with the chaperones, sure she can handle it and not cross any lines, the stories will fly straight to the Voy boards, no matter what the truth is.

Sure enough, most of the girls are not asleep yet when a post rings out on the Tabloids board a few minutes after ten P.M. on their first night in D.C.:

*OMG the Fur queen, Sugar queen and Yam
queen just left the Washington hotel for the
Mardi Gras ball with one of the male chaperones. Way start a reputation on your first night
in D.C.*

Because they are actually busy enjoying their trip, none of
the girls in D.C. see the post when it first appears. But plenty
of people in Louisiana read it and respond, claims and coun-
terclaims flying back and forth all night, even as the same
post—clearly by someone with an ax to grind—appears in
modified version on the Fair and Positive board, newly clari-
fied to say the author meant Fur, Sugar, and Cotton, who was
an *old* Yam queen.

That distinction—revealing a knowledge of Brandy's rhinestone history—makes it clear that the author is a festival person. By breakfast on Thursday, the queens have heard about
the post and have joined a two-pronged debate already stretching pages long on the boards: Did the girls in question even do
it, and who was bitchy enough to post their whereabouts,
anyway?

Lauren and Brandy wake up to this news, and neither of
them is happy about it. They know immediately what gave
birth to this story. Last night, Lauren and Brandy were chatting in the hotel lobby just as a swarm of chaperones (and not
just male ones) headed out for a late dinner and drinks. When
the chaperones invited the girls to join them, the trio said
they couldn't, not just because of the rules, but because they

were waiting to meet Lauren's mom and boss, Nicky, for drinks in the hotel lounge. To be honest, Lauren would have loved to go out on the town—she's a college senior, not a little kid, and she was in a world-class city instead of back home. She'd watched a little ruefully as the crowd disappeared into the night.

To learn that she's been pegged as a rule-breaker anyway is maddening. "If I had gone anywhere, with or without a guy, I could see it, but my mom was around all night long." Lauren's mom would be happy to vouch for the girls, except that it would be pointless: Their accuser is unknown and most of the audience for the story is back in Louisiana. The inability to face her critics makes Lauren furious. "What's my mom gonna do? Write a note on the boards? *That'll* help."

Brandy could cry. For a girl who barely dates, to be turned into the subject of a suggestive story feels unfair. Worse, as she's hoping to reclaim her spot in the Top 15 at Queen of Queens, she knows a story like this could come back to haunt her. But what can she do? As one of only two girls with no parent in D.C., she doesn't even have that shoulder to lean on.

Kristen would be more sympathetic to both, except that she feels they shouldn't have been drinking even in the hotel, where everyone can see them. As they're of legal age, what they drink when not wearing crown and banner is their business, but she still thinks their deportment was unwise in this particular setting, with or without regalia.

Chelsea is rooming with the Shrimp Queen, and when the rumors reach them, Shrimp logs on to her computer to seek out the story on the Voy board. Chelsea's throat tightens up and her heart races: If Shrimp hasn't seen the DWI arrest story before, she's sure to see it now. "I'm thinking, 'I'm not the most religious person but, God, if you remember me, kill her Internet connection!'" God may not be willing to dabble in earthly affairs that much, but the connection is indeed slow, and Chelsea takes the opportunity to break the story herself. Her roommate is genuinely surprised—she hadn't yet heard it through the Rhinestone grapevine. But she assures Chelsea that she doesn't think ill of her, then hops back online to find out the current dish.

The girls spend the rest of Thursday and all of Friday doing two things: touring the capital and texting about the Voy boards. Kristen, in an eye-popping cow-print winter coat, focuses on the sights. "Our guide knows every language in creation. We name a language, and he begins speaking in it. I'm jealous. I'm not even good at speaking perfect English grammar."

The 365 steps to the Capitol are quite a hike in heels, which all the queens wear with their interview suits, but the real challenge for Louisiana girls is the cold. Not used to temperatures in the teens, they are happy for every moment inside, including visits to their representatives, like Congressman Charlie Melancon (who Lauren says makes a better impression than Jindal), and to the home of Senator Mary Landrieu, the first female captain of the Mystick Krewe. When the senator is called away to vote on the stimulus package that has been dominating the headlines for days, the girls have a chance to play in the snow on Landrieu's lawn. Though the opportunity for such winter fun doesn't arise back home, only a few dare brave the freezing air again to enjoy it. Kristen moans afterward, "I think I gave myself frostbite in my fingers . . . way too cold!"

No matter where they go, the Voy board rumors stay close behind, following them back to the hotel. Chelsea is relieved not to be the subject this time, but she's also rattled by how intensely the board gets followed. "Most of the girls have stayed on their phones all day looking at what's being posted, even in the Capitol. We're all sitting down for dinner and everyone at my table is texting or Voy-board surfing." One of the things that bothers her most is that girls seem to be texting about other girls at the table right under one another's noses. Friday at lunch, someone shows Chelsea a text about Queen Sugar, who is sitting just a couple of seats away, oblivious. Chelsea stops talking and picks at her plate. A few of her fellow queens had reached out to her after her arrest, making her feel as if they were on her side, but the behavior at this table casts doubt on such assurances, and her guard goes back up.

After a number of queens in D.C. post on the Voy board that the girls in question never left the hotel, much of the online discussion turns to the motives of the original poster: Does she have a personal grudge? Was it the outgrowth of the tension between festivals that never get to go to D.C. and those that do, an attempt to unseat a regular and open up a new slot? One respondent suggests the woman is just crazy, and writes, *"Ask the voices in her head! Ask the voices!"*

Why *does* anyone care whether three girls (two of legal drinking age and all over the age of consent) are not in bed by ten P.M., rules or no rules? In some ways, it's a sign of our culturewide obsession with the lives of the famous, even if the famous in this case are public figures paid in three figures. We've grown accustomed to paparazzi stalking celebrities, bloggers feeding us endless dish on stars' private lives. Louisiana festival queens get the full treatment: From their choice of photos on MySpace to the dresses they wear at a ball to how enthusiastically they shuck oysters at a festival, every action becomes fair game for public discussion. At a certain point, they can't help but wonder: *Who is it that sits up all night recording a queen's every move and dissecting her royal conduct?*

Whoever it was, "she" is now a "they," and groups are battling for and against the girls' reputations online. Some of the posters really have it in for their subjects. The threads have left the original claim and turned more and more to personal attacks, first that the girls in question are "old" queens who have stayed around too long, and then that they are secretly mean girls who "aren't as nice as you think" and "deserve a turn" to be smeared.

While Lauren and Brandy react to the charges variously with anger and sadness, the third subject, Queen Sugar, seems to have decided to flip a bird at the Voy community, fanning the flames with a "Give 'em what they came for" approach. She jokes with the younger chaperones in the hallways, always managing to land a hand on this one's firm bicep or that one's back, and she acts as though she doesn't care who minds. It's a risky gambit and sets tongues wagging even more. Is it chicken or egg? Did the flirting come first and get reported, or did the reporting make her decide she might as well flirt? Either way, Sugar almost dares you to notice.

The currents of this drama subside somewhat as the girls gather during Saturday's orientation session for the Grand Ball. Dapper silver-haired Joe Broussard, senior lieutenant of the Mystick Krewe of Louisianians, takes the podium and scans the roomful of crowns and tiaras. At seventy-two, he's been ringmaster of D.C. Mardi Gras for thirty-two years, and has been attending it—albeit, initially with a babysitter—since his father helped found it in 1945.

This morning, he addresses the girls who have been selected to serve as the official sparkle of a ball not short on it. Two sets of royalty will appear tonight: a total of sixty-one princesses and queens. The princesses, thirty-six of them, are the daughters, granddaughters, and nieces of prominent Louisianians, and they will promenade before the seated crowd, each girl clad in white and entering on the arm of her tuxedo-clad male relative. But the twenty-five festival queens trump them: Unescorted, they come in last, no two dressed alike, each basking alone in the spotlight. Queens have been part of the action since 1945, with Yam the only queen who has been invited every single year. Being here is huge for the current Yambilee Queen, who has never been farther north than Missouri. She is not alone in this regard: Several of the queens have never left the state. All the girls know it's a privilege to be here, and that Joe expects them to live up to it.

This morning, there is a clear division between the princesses and the festival queens. The festival girls sit front and center together in four rows, a unit, while the princesses—many of whom have never met before and for whom this identity is only one weekend long—sit toward the sides and the back in clusters of one or two, sometimes three or four. Each princess wears a delicate little tiara. It would lend a girl a magical air in any context but this one, where it looks like a practice crown in the shadow of the queens' headwear.

The princesses don't seem to mind that visual distinction; most of them are girls of privilege, not Ag girls, and some overtly roll their eyes at the festival titles—Farm Bureau Queen? Queen Verengeria of the Order of the Troubadours? When the emcee asks the princesses to verify the names of the escorts for him to read tonight, they are quick to make sure that no ceremonial title is missed: "The Honorable . . ." and "Commissioner . . ." and "Representative . . . ," not to mention Doctor This and Doctor That.

In contrast, the queens emphasize their *festival* titles, making sure the emcee gets them exactly right; after all, this is one of the most high-profile moments of their year as spokeswomen. What's good enough in casual conversation won't cut it tonight. When the emcee says "Frog Festival," Chelsea corrects him in a firm voice: "*Rayne* Frog Festival," making sure he doesn't omit the town she loves. And the Orange Queen has to nudge him a couple of times to get in her entire title:

"Plaquemines Parish Fair and Orange Festival Queen 62," which not only identifies the what but the where and even the how long—a lesson in geography and history in eight words.

Once they've received their instructions, Joe releases the queens with an admonition: "You're the stars, so *act* like it!" A few girls laugh nervously. He doesn't know that some of them have been accused of following that advice too literally and are now facing the kind of tabloid treatment that a movie star would understand.

Now free to go anywhere they like until the main event, Kristen, Brandy, Chelsea, and Lauren slip away from the hotel for lunch in a nearby inn. The twenty-item menu includes gumbo and po'boys, neither of which the girls would dream of eating this far north. Brandy orders first: a hamburger with Cheddar and fries. And then Kristen orders it, too. As does Lauren. When Chelsea orders the exact same thing, even the waitress has to laugh. It's not a joke or some group-think experiment: They've just had so much fancy food in four days that they're sick of it. "I've been dreaming about a burger since Thursday," Kristen sighs happily.

The conversation ranges from Governor Jindal (four thumbs down) to the chaperones (thumbs up on looks, down on behavior) and ends up on Queen of Queens, now exactly a week away. Throughout the meal, Chelsea grows ever quieter, her hands falling still in her lap, her eyes less and less frequently meeting those of her peers. All the talk of the competition ahead just brings up anxiety about her arrest. Will she have any chance of doing well if the story is widespread by the time she arrives? And what are other queens saying about her at lunches like this all over town? By the time the check comes, she's ready for a break from the group, eager to head out for an afternoon of shopping with her predecessors Brooke and Charmaine, which should help take her mind off things.

At the mall, Chelsea is looking at handbags when the arrest drama catches up with her again. Talking about how evil the Voy boards are, Brooke says, "I draw the line at them using my sister." Chelsea goes cold; this is the first she has heard of today's post: a new salvo that suggests that the Frog Queen is living it up and partying in D.C., and that it is shameful for Brooke, in light of her sister's death, to be there supporting Chelsea. It's a nakedly cruel post, which has just the effect the author seems to have intended: It wounds everyone involved. Both are starting to wonder if their efforts are worth it.

When the long-awaited hour comes, shadows dispel and spirits rise. An event that has survived wars, recessions past and present, and all manner of cultural shifts, the Grand Ball lives up to its billing. The richness of Louisiana culture is on full display, elevating the girls past their troubles for a few hours. It is impossible to resist the cry of Mardi Gras, *"Laissez les bon temps rouler"*—Let the good times roll!

While guests in black tie and designer cocktail dresses

stream through the hotel, drinks in hand, elegant ensembles topped with beads and feathers and blinking-light necklaces, the queens are gathered in their waiting area, an ocean of regalia: rhinestone whitecaps riding silk waves above a velvet seabed. The Southwest Mardi Gras Queen is so tall that her crown catches on a chandelier. Creole Gumbo goes by with her mom close behind, lifting her daughter's heavy train and sighing with fatigue from the effort. Crawfish shows up for pictures in a white dress cut up to her thigh and then rushes back upstairs to change into red, because too many other girls are in white. As she hurries away, she purrs that she brought an outfit in every color for this exact reason.

Orange and Rice stand together comparing gowns. Rice is wearing a silky green dress that she had made just to match the colors in her train. Orange, in ivory, is wearing the same dress as every other Orange queen. This is not just a figurative statement: The outgoing queen wears a vintage silk gown to the pageant that crowns her successor; that very gown is passed on to the next queen that night, even before the pageant is officially over. Hinged and trussed and loaded with the clothing equivalent of trapdoors, it is a marvel of engineering: The bust expands or contracts by seven inches, the sides can be cinched or let out, and the hem can fall or rise by a foot. A five-foot-eleven, 120-pound outgoing queen can crown a five-foot-three, 190-pound girl, whisk her away from the stage for a dress handoff, and then return just minutes later with the successor looking fabulous. It's a gown designed for a world in which Kate Moss and Oprah Winfrey swap clothes.

Men in dark suits roam the halls, earpieces with rubber tendrils trailing into shirts. With so many senators and Congresspeople in attendance, it makes sense. Rumor has it that Vice President Biden might show, too. One person not here is Governor Jindal, who attended last year and, according to the newspapers, poured champagne in the state hospitality suite. His absence is much-discussed among the guests milling about the ballroom—some think he's afraid it would make him look insensitive to be seen living it up despite the terrible economy, but others argue that D.C. Mardi Gras is like Christmas: You can scale back how you celebrate, but you absolutely cannot take it off the calendar (especially if you're a first-term governor). Jindal's absence is a hot enough topic that his press secretary has defended him to a Louisiana newspaper by saying that the governor did his part already by hosting the queens at the mansion.

At last, it is time for the Grand Ball, which occurs in a vast space composed of conjoined ballrooms filling nearly an entire floor of the hotel. Imagine an arena rock concert mixed with a carnival and a black-tie reception and you can begin to sense what it's like. Colored lights sweep the massive space, illuminating several thousand alcohol-fueled revelers, society mavens waving light-up toys like children at a circus, captains of industry donning iridescent beads over their tuxedos. The dominant color is purple, the ceiling lit like a plum sky. The happy throngs are captured by roaming camera crews and displayed overhead on Jumbotron screens, so that guests at one end can see the others partying hearty five hundred tables away.

There are more people in this room than live in the entire town of Basile, where Swine takes place, and the din of their conversation roars off all the hard surfaces, concrete and metal, so that everything must be said more and more loudly, the decibels rising continually even before the first band plays. A Dixieland combo struts through the aisles with a peppy Louis Armstrong rhythm, hips and trumpets swaying, while rainbow-hued confetti fills the air in a Technicolor sandstorm. The crowd roars approval, their cries swelling in waves of happiness. The house orchestra takes its turn, blasting swing-dance numbers to the distant rafters. And we've only just begun: Here comes the Marine band from Quantico, navy-clad wooden soldiers marching through the arena with perfect precision, the vast hall throbbing with approval.

As if three live bands were not enough to whip up a frenzy, what had seemed to be the back wall of the ballroom stage splits in half, revealing a double-decker float, topped by a crown-shaped carriage inside of which sits the new King of Mardi Gras. (This year's monarch heads up several timber and mineral resources corporations.) He rises to acknowledge the full-throated hollering of his new subjects. Soon he is joined on his gilded perch by his daughter, whom he has selected as the new Mardi Gras Queen. The Jumbotron shows the look of love that she gives him as he reaches out his hand to welcome her aboard the float. The first father-daughter royal duo ever, they are both beaming.

The emcee tries to quiet the crowd to reveal a surprise. As a special thank-you to the Mystick Krewe, the new king has arranged for unprecedented special guests to join them—the LSU Tiger Marching Band. The emcee tries to stretch out the band's name to heighten the impact, but the crowd loses its collective mind at the letters "LSU." It is like a joy bomb goes off: The screaming exceeds anything heard all night, and grown men leap onto their chairs to get a better view. There is no way to overstate how much Cajuns love the Tigers, and the LSU band has been treated like rock stars since before there even *were* rock stars. When the Rice Festival booked the band seventy years ago, it drew tens of thousands of people even then. Tonight I can hear the Tigers—a fighting cadence rings out across the arena—but I cannot see them past several thousand revelers in the way, their cell-phone cameras held aloft, a waving field of high-tech wheat. The Tigers finally come into view: Golden Girl dancers and drum majors followed by brass and percussion clad in sharp gold-and-black uniforms, their band caps crowned by white plumes bobbing like a phalanx of egrets.

From box seats behind velvet ropes, the elite of Louisiana reach out to the Tigers like sick people trying to touch the hems of saints. For some, that's not good enough. Two well-heeled women edge closer and closer to the action, leaning into the aisle until a beanpole of a guard tries to steer them back to their seats. When they demand to know who he thinks he is, he makes the mistake of saying he is working security, and when pressed further, he admits that, yes, this is his first ball. "Well, we've been coming for twenty-five years, buddy," barks a corpulent blonde, her angry face the same iodine shade as her dress, "and *we're* not moving." He gives them an incredulous look: *They have to be kidding.* But he's just a guard and they're red-hot Cajun mamas—who do you think prevails?

Decorum is restored as the princesses are presented, now an hour and a half into the evening. The crowds return to their seats, ordering new drinks, to toast the procession as girl after girl enters, each in a white ball gown and elbow gloves. As the girls' towns and parishes are named, they receive bursts of applause from their fellow citizens sitting in this or that corner of the arena. They navigate a track that both outlines the audience and cuts through it like a canal, a figure-eight loop that ends with them promenading up the middle to reserved seats on the stage to the right of the king and queen. Most princesses are white, but a few girls of color are among them, one of whom earns the loudest applause, perhaps because she has *the* most princesslike name ever: Qianna Monique Champagne.

At long last, it is time for the entry of the festival queens, the ultimate dignitaries whose arrival and seating will signal the time for the Grand Parade to begin. The queens took formal portraits at five P.M., long before the ball even started, and have been ready to go ever since. Imagine waiting four hours to make an entrance, clad the entire time in high heels, a metal mantle, and a ten-pound cape that stretches as much as a dozen feet behind you. Though the queens are eager to take their first steps, it not an overstatement to say that some of them are now so stiff, their muscles so cramped, that they can barely move.

Costumed men guide their way, one at every corner, steering them toward the next turn in the maze. Each queen is led by her own Krewe member, a random stranger assigned to clear her path. There are hundreds of Krewe members at this event, most dressed in colorful silks, their faces masked, some with capes or feathered headdresses. There is no strict rule as to what they must wear, so Kristen finds herself walking behind what looks like a drunken Elvis impersonator in a red belted jumpsuit and a pompadour that has not yet been tamed; it's both a little startling and a lot hilarious when she recognizes him as a politician from her parish. She walks confidently, pausing at corners of the maze for photos, the same black-and-ivory gown she wore during her Cattle parade now the perfect evening outfit.

Brandy's white gown falls in five billowy layers split in the front, so that each step forward parts the waves of fabric. She has to hang back a bit, sometimes darting a little to one side or the other, because her Krewe member is prancing around, waving to friends, and doing funny little dance steps, all without seeming to remember that he is carrying an enormous, sharp-edged sign on a pole that swings behind him at Brandy's head. It is up to her to avoid losing a crown—or an eye—as her escort mindlessly flings the placard. Even so, to hear her name called, to see the crowds of strangers giving her their attention, makes her feel like a true queen.

In a hip-hugging hourglass gown of white with silver trim, Lauren strides through the maze faster than any of her peers, no small feat since she is the shortest queen here. There is nothing tentative about Lauren—she's done this three times before and she walks like she owns the place. When Fur is announced as her festival, she earns some of the loudest cheers all night, and her perfect queen smile gives way to a broad grin of unstudied pride.

Brooke and Charmaine, both of them having made this walk themselves, have told Chelsea to just soak in the moment of her entrance, that people love the Frog Queen. She hopes so, because it's been a bad month and she's been looking forward to this moment so much that she won't be able to stand it if it goes poorly. The pain of scoliosis has been ramped up by the hours strapped into her mantle and train, so she's sore all over as she prepares to take her first step forward in her slim green gown with black beading. A happy roar rises to the rafters when the emcee gets to her name and announces her as the Rayne Frog Queen, and at least for this one hour, it feels easy and good to be that girl.

This is the magic of D.C. Mardi Gras for a festival queen. All the gossip, all the drama, all the attempts to make this girl or that one look good or bad before next week's Queen of Queens—it's swept away by the sheer energy of the ball. This is the hour that these girls have heard so many tales about, and to their joy, it is everything they imagined. How many of us will ever know what it's like to bask in the heat of a spotlight following our every step as thousands of strangers rise to their feet cheering at the mere sight of us? It is an overwhelming thing, a rush that erases everything else for a time. The hospital ward where Lauren watched her sister fight for her life? Gone. The dark room where Kristen lay huddled in a ball unable to get a doctor's appointment? Gone. The scales that told Brandy she wasn't who she wanted to be? Gone. The sheriff by the dark road to Rayne? Gone. Family fights, double shifts, breakups, the miserable soul-killing Voy boards, all gone. For the rest of their lives, they will have this moment. Even as this gem of memory grows ever smaller against the crowded landscape of years, it will still glow inside them, a thrilling instant when they were shining in their own light. Like stars.

15

And One Remains

It is Thursday evening in Baton Rouge, Louisiana's second-largest city, and the first floor of the Crowne Plaza Executive Center looks like an Oprah Winfrey audience: Women of all ages stream down the main hall toward the ballrooms, talking about how exciting it is to be here. It's almost time to begin orientation for Queen of Queens, the pageant taking place over the next three days in tandem with the annual Louisiana Association of Fairs and Festivals Convention. The hotel carpeting mutes the noise of foot traffic as eighty-six girls, along with their mothers and their pageant directors, fill one of the smaller ballrooms, nearly three hundred people crowding in for this meeting.

Rare is the event where so many Miss Queens are together at once; even the biggest turnouts, such as the one hundred queens who attended the Frog crowning, are composed of a mix of Teen and Junior and Ms. royalty together. This pageant is the one place where Miss queens can count on seeing the greatest number of their Rhinestone Sisters, and they embrace one another like long-lost siblings, praising new hairstyles and outfits, asking about boys and school. Directors compare notes on how their queens have been doing, while Queen Moms commiserate over road trip stories.

Tonight is only part reunion, however; it's also part reconnaissance. Discreetly, girls and parents alike are sizing up the competition. Who stands out? Who looks good? Who seems most comfortable? Everyone knows it is pointless to speculate: With eighty-six girls competing, it is harder to win this pageant than to win Miss America or Miss Universe. Yet it is impossible to come to a pageant without playing the "Which girl?" game.

There is a lot of talk about a somewhat more attainable goal: making the Top 15. (Even those odds are long, seeing as seventy-one girls will not.) Kristen sees both pride and peril in landing a top spot. "Top Fifteen makes you proud of yourself while you're representing your festival and making them proud. But once you've made Top Fifteen, you have *way* more pressure if you go back the next year."

That's exactly what Brandy is feeling. Having made Top 15 at only nineteen, in her first try, it was painful when she failed to repeat the same feat at twenty. After her year out of the sisterhood, she wants to reclaim her spot and prove that the first red pin was not a fluke. But with this being her last turn on the runway, she also admits that she'd like to aim higher: "This year the goal is Top Five even. And the more I think about wanting that, the more I want to be Queen of Queens and have the job of representing our entire state!"

Less enthusiastic is Chelsea, who sits quietly on a folding chair near the front of the room. She's been told that the LAFF president had wanted Ms. Cheryl to bar her from competing, but Ms. Cheryl had explained to him that LAFF's contract was the model upon which the original Frog contract had been based. If the president didn't want Chelsea at Queen of Queens, he'd have to tell Chelsea himself and see whether he fared any better than the chamber had. He passed on that opportunity. There is something amazing about the fact that, when push came to shove, the president of a hundred-festival system doesn't dare mess with a ninety-five-pound girl who stands just over five feet tall and speaks in a voice soft as a breeze through tall grass. Even so, Chelsea assumes this makes her persona non grata to the LAFF board, and she is determined to conduct herself in a way that makes Rayne look good in the face of all the recent controversy. "Honestly, my focus this weekend is to get to Sunday alive."

The lack of a welcome mat would be enough to tamp her down, but there is one more element: Angie and Ms. Cheryl have asked Chelsea to get up before all the queens and apologize. She can't be required to do this (the chamber now fully aware how precise a contract is), and everyone involved knows that to make such a speech will just about feel like death to her. She has gone over the merits of speaking or not speaking a thousand times in her head: Why inform all the queens who haven't yet heard? Will it make any real difference to those who disapprove of her? Or will her confession so doom her from the start of the weekend that it's not worth being here? But she has agreed to speak, even if it means the rest of the girls treat her like a leper, because she truly believes in her heart that the most important thing she can do right now is heal the damage with her town. Queen of Queens is nothing next to the chance to show Rayne that, short of slinking away in defeat, she'll do anything to serve her festival.

The LAFF pageant director quiets the crowd. Chelsea, who has already spent most of her day alternating between crying and throwing up, feels her stomach muscles tighten. Waving a manila folder of orientation materials, the director indicates that the Miss Rayne Frog Festival Queen has something she'd like to say. Chelsea rises, trying to square her bird-like shoulders, and walks to the front. She just wants to be done, so she can head back to her room as quickly as she's allowed. She is supposed to stay for a fifties-themed "Drive-In Party" tonight, but she's planning to skip it, convinced this speech will make her a pariah.

She is barely audible as she introduces herself, and the room stills to a dead hush to listen. Her eyes are focused on a tiny slip of paper, upon which she has written a similarly tiny speech. She can't look at her fellow queens, and the paper flutters in nervous fingers, but her voice gets clearer, firmer word by word. She says how sorry she is for letting them all down, but also how grateful to still be able to call herself Frog Queen, and that she hopes her Rhinestone Sisters will support her as she works hard to represent her festival for the remaining months. In under a hundred words, she has satisfied

Ms. Cheryl and Angie by offering an apology that doesn't contain an excuse, while serving notice to her critics that she isn't going anywhere, and personally calling for her Rhinestone Sisters to close ranks around her. There is only a half-breath of silence in the room when she finishes, and then applause from her fellow queens closes the distance between her and them.

When she slides back into her seat, color is creeping into her cheeks, but there is also the first hint of a smile. And when orientation is over, some of the girls—including queens she hasn't even yet met—take time to approach her. There is no hostility in the air, no hint of scorn: Most of her Rhinestone Sisters seem to have accepted her apology at face value. One of them, Miss Beauregard Parish Fair (known as Beau Fair), is a teenager from halfway across the state, and though she doesn't know Chelsea, she's impressed. "It takes a lot of courage to be a girl who doesn't hide her mistakes!"

A change comes over Chelsea, a physical lightness. "Some girls are telling me, 'Thank you for doing that,' and I'm like, 'Thank *me*? Thank *you* for coming up!' " Everything about her face, her posture, how her hands move, is less pinched than before the meeting. Her tone brightens. "Maybe I'll stay for the party after all."

The business of picking a queen begins in earnest Friday morning as girls assemble in groups of five for their make-or-break offstage interviews. There are five judges this year, and they each have a table of their own behind closed cream-colored ballroom doors. Each quintet of queens is ushered into the room, where they sit one queen to a judge for their first question, then, on cue, shift one table to their left for the next judge, rotating round-robin until the pageant version of a speed-dating session has paired up all possible combinations. To get through all the interviews will take six or seven hours. (That's a good thing because Kristen has to drive to campus to take a two-hour exam and then drive back to this hotel before her slot.)

As is the case at all pageant interviews, contestants wear "business attire," which is to say skirted suit ensembles, and the going trend is vivid color: peacock blue, lipstick red, electric salmon. The few girls in black may be regretting it—they look instantly aged in context, dour when they need to be selling cheer. Even with so many colors to pick from, it is hard to stand out in *any* suit if eighty-five other girls are also wearing one, but Brandy manages to carve out her own niche with a soft white suit that makes her olive skin and black hair read as exotic. When Chelsea appears, it is clear that she either didn't get the memo or didn't care to read it: She looks stunning in a sleek hot-pink sweater dress with a white sixties-style belt. Whether this will make the judges swoon or go blind all depends on whether they prefer personality or conformity.

Clothing isn't the primary concern, anyway. The real issue is how the girls handle the questions, and as the first few sets of contestants come out, it is clear that some of today's queries are not what they were expecting. At their home festivals, where they must prepare all kinds of lore about local crops or historic events, it is easy to get a handle on the material; here, with judges mostly from out of state, no such thing is possible. But this year's judges are also disconnected from the festival system at large; in an attempt to select the least biased judges, LAFF has found judges with backgrounds more connected to Miss USA, Miss America, and the entertainment industry. As a result, the girls find themselves answering more general lifestyle questions. Worse, the single most dreaded interview topic is apparently taking center stage: Some of the judges are asking about politics.

In an election year, that probably shouldn't have surprised anyone, but the questions being asked of the girls go beyond simple red-state/blue-state queries. Brandy is startled when a male judge looks her in the eye and asks if she thinks Obama got elected just because he's black. The right answer for a queen speaking of the president of the United States is no (followed by something lyrical and inoffensive), but the question itself is so harsh, she must also pause to consider whether that answer might anger a judge who himself secretly thinks "yes." Brandy smiles sweetly and follows the "no" route but very, very gently.

Girl after girl, the contestants come out wearing expressions of shock at some of the questions. Would you have an abortion? What should Louisiana do about all the Mexicans coming to the state? Who's more racist, white people or black people? Presumably, the rationale of the judges is that lobbing such incendiary questions allows them to see how well a girl reacts under pressure, her actual answer less revealing than her demeanor while giving it. After she's finished, one queen steps into the hallway and grabs her director's arm, whispering loudly, "Ma'am, that was a train wreck!"

And yet others return from interview feeling pretty good—they kept their smiles on, hid any alarm, and said things that didn't sound too stupid. Kristen and Brandy both feel they did well. Kristen loves to talk, was *born* to, and has only one setting—herself—so the judges got the same natural answers she'd have given her friends. And despite the Obama shocker, Brandy says, "I had an awesome interview. It's good to feel like the judges got to see and know a little bit about the real me."

Chelsea is four-fifths of the way through her round-robin when a female judge greets her with a statement, not a question: "I think you should know that I'm from Louisiana." Before Chelsea can reply, the judge continues. "From New Iberia." Chelsea understands immediately what she is hearing: New Iberia is a half hour away from Rayne. Like Rayne and a host of small towns, New Iberia is one of the towns in the *Advertiser* newspaper chain, which published the report of Chelsea's arrest. LAFF may easily find non-festival judges, but it can hardly pick judges who have agreed not to read a newspaper for the previous year.

Chelsea leaves the room neither bitter nor especially doubtful. "I have no shot whatsoever of making Top Fifteen." In a way, this belief frees her. She makes a joke about doing whatever she wants now, and it's the first time in a while that I've heard her laugh.

In keeping with this year's convention theme, LAFF Goes to Hollywood, Friday night's main event is a costumed banquet at which all the contestants must dress in outfits from the world of film and television. Tonight is the first time the girls will be presented to the convention-goers at large, each contestant introducing herself to hundreds of festival board members from all over Louisiana who are here competing for prizes of their own, including Best Event and Professional of the Year.

To the tune of "Diamonds Are a Girl's Best Friend," the queens parade in, their own mini Mardi Gras of colorful costumes. There are perhaps a half dozen Dorothys from *The Wizard of Oz,* one of whom wisely brought a live Toto in a basket to make herself stand out. That isn't the only duplicate by a long shot: There are twinned Scarlett O'Haras, Cleopatras, and Cruellas, as well as Wonder Women and Minnie Mice and Pocahonti. Months ago, Kristen chose her identity: Jessie the Cowgirl from *Toy Story 2,* figuring she would be the only cow-related queen at the pageant; but damn if there isn't another girl in the exact same outfit, anyway. Good sports both, they laugh it off and praise each other's attire. A few steps away, Cajun Food poses with Beau Fair for pictures as the grande and venti versions of Marilyn Monroe.

Cochon de Lait (whose title refers to a suckling pig) may

be taking an aesthetic risk by donning a snout as Miss Piggy—will a judge ever be able to see her any other way now?—but at least she has managed to reflect her festival in her costume. Chelsea has, as well: She wears a green-and-gold sequined leotard with a black tux and top hat as Michigan J. Frog, the logo for the former WB Network.

Brandy has pulled off a hat trick: She wears an outfit that flatters her, that no one else is wearing, *and* that somehow manages to gently invoke Cotton, a title that doesn't lend itself easily to costumes. Wearing the color white is about all a Cotton Queen can do to sell her theme in any circumstance, so Brandy has chosen the *Star Wars* heroine Princess Leia, who wears the best-known all-white outfit in cinema. The hip-hugging pantsuit is flattering and unlike any other queen's costume, which should make this a triumph, but Brandy looks tired and her smile is not convincing. In the hours since interview, she has developed a head cold that has near-completely stolen her voice and made every step woozy. "I went from feeling like I was on cloud nine this morning to feeling like I'm floating on that cloud from all the medicine I'm taking."

When all the queens have been introduced, it is time for current Queen of Queens Brandi Stout to have her say. The other girls were warned months in advance that the one character they *absolutely* couldn't be tonight was Holly Golightly, because one of the outgoing queen's perks is the right to reserve one costume for herself alone. Brandi is the picture of elegance, hair swept up, arms robed in silk gloves, her smile radiant. When she takes the microphone off the stand and starts chatting with the audience, the difference in poise and control between her and the queens vying to replace her is profound. It is clear what a full year as spokeswoman for LAFF can do for a girl; she could take off her tiara and run for office now if she wanted to.

The introductions give way to live music, including a band that plays "Jessie's Girl" and "Summer of '69" on zydeco accordion, but the queens are the real entertainment. They were told beforehand that it is their job tonight to be seen having fun, playing pep squad for the convention-goers, and so they do. While Elle Woods boogies with the band, Tracy Turnblad grooves so hard that she nearly falls off the stage. Hannah Montana and her doppelgänger, Miley Cyrus, make devil horns during "Every Rose Has Its Thorn," and, beyond them, the feathers of a Cruella De Vil can be seen keeping the beat. Down front, the Cat tries not to lose her Hat.

It is hours before the costume party is over and the crowds spill from the stifling ballroom into the lobby. The heat has taken a toll on a lot of girls, who are dying to ditch their costumes. Brandy heads off to bed almost immediately, and Kristen says she thinks she's coming down with something, too, but she doesn't head upstairs right away because there are too many people to see. The ground floor of the hotel is like one big party right now, with various festivals setting up camp in corners of the bar or outside on the patio. Male board members from Duck, dressed as the cast of *M*A*S*H,* are running around passing out lime-green Jell-O shots, first in syringes, and then as the evening progresses, in specimen cups.

Chelsea quietly takes this all in. As festival directors down shots, and the level of public drunkenness around her grows with every passing minute, it is hard for her to understand how people could have judged her so harshly. Drinking is not at all unusual for a convention; all over the world, people attend conventions for the express purpose of being able to cut loose with like-minded folk. But for a girl in Chelsea's position, there is no way to feel anything but burned by this hotel-sized keg party led by the same people she is meant to respect and emulate.

When Kristen gets to her room at midnight, she makes a horrible discovery: There is a stain of some kind right on the front of her competition gown. Telling her not to worry, that it'll come right out, her aunt unwisely takes soap and water to it—which turns the silk white, not just where the stain is, but where a splash of water hits the skirt below the hip. Kristen calls her dad in a panic, hoping he'll grab her other dress and drive two hours with it—this is love!—but when he answers, bleary and sniffling, it's clear he's sick. It'll have to be this dress. The aunt redeems herself, pulling some of the original embroidery off the waistband and tacking it over the stain in front. But the same trick won't do for hiding the second spot: There's no way a lone bit of appliqué floating off on one hip will fool anybody, so the aunt does the next best thing, pinning Kristen's contestant number over the blemish. At last, with her own cold worsening, Kristen calls it a night.

. . .

Saturday is the longest and final day, and by nightfall, the girls
are both keyed up and exhausted at the same time. Things officially started with registration for evening gown prelims
back at eight A.M. in a side ballroom. But for many of the
contestants, the day actually started before sunrise, as friends,
mothers, or professional hairdressers cajoled their tresses into
the new version of "big hair," which is less about vertical rise
and more about downward, outward swoop. As the girls prepared, the Sawmill Queen went room to room on the contestants' floor, knocking and pausing at each door before
cheerily calling out, "Good morning and good luck," revealing herself to be either the sweetest girl ever or a savvy strate-
gist with her sights set on winning Miss Congeniality. The
rest of the morning was spent competing in the evening
gown prelims, a three-hour show in which the girls were
judged on their poise as they modeled in the same gowns
they will wear during the final competition tonight.

Now the sun has set, and the hour has come. Or, I sup-
pose, the four hours, because there are no brief events at
LAFF. Two ballrooms have been combined and decorated
cinematically. The stage—backed by the famous Hollywood
sign—is hot with the glow of spotlights. Many dozens of
round tables are squeezed together on either side of a grand
aisle stretching the length of both ballrooms. Beneath pointed-
shard chandeliers, teen queens in festival banners and crowns
sit side by side with farmers in John Deere caps and cowboy

boots; older women dolled up in mother-of-the-bride attire share tables with young men in half-unbuttoned nightclub shirts. *Everyone* is here.

Across the hall, the assembled queens battle nerves and remind themselves that it will all be over soon. Chelsea may be the most relaxed girl present; she feels like she has nothing to lose. She chats with Crawfish, whom she got to know in D.C., and they make a plan to go out to eat when the pageant is over and they can be themselves again. Kristen isn't her bubbly self at all; the cold she felt coming on the night before is suddenly so intense that she is sweating and nauseous, *not* the impression she hoped to make tonight. She thinks of her dad's exhausted voice on the phone last night and wonders: *Is that how* I *sound?*

Cold medicine helps keep Brandy going, but she is also buoyed by the reception she received this morning at evening gown prelims. Even though she was one of the first contestants onstage, she remained the subject of audible buzz even when it was over. "The girl in the green at the beginning," said one woman to her companion, "she's so pretty. There's just something *about* her." Another couple at prelims intently scanned the pageant program trying to find Brandy, asking, "Who *was* that?" All day, strangers approached her to say that they hoped she'd win. One woman even asked if she could get an autograph before the pageant so she wouldn't have to wait in line with everyone else afterward. This really touches Brandy. "They know who I am and what I represent. It's incredible to know that so many people think so highly of me, especially since I feel like crap! And it kind of helps to soften the harshness of the mean things said about me in D.C."

But this praise comes with an inescapable burden: high expectations. There's no way to hear all day that she might actually win without it doing a number on her psyche. What if she doesn't even place? "Now there's tons of pressure to make it back into the top this year," she says. "I can feel what people expect from me."

There's no such pressure on Lauren. Fur's boycott of LAFF means that she's sitting at one of the round banquet tables tonight as a spectator, while friends like Brandy and Yam Queen Meghin are in the greenroom preparing for their entrances. Like Brandy, Meghin is possessed of two red pins already, and she's been the subject of intense chatter today. Unable to compete herself, Lauren considers her friends' chances instead. Complicated calculations take place behind her blue eyes, before she shakes her head, unable to make a prediction. "I just don't know. Some years there are clear favorites, girls you just know are gonna win. This year, Meghin is going to do well. And Brandy, too, everyone's talking about her. But some years the winner just comes out of nowhere. No one had ever heard of Tamale last year and she won. I think it's still wide open."

With just moments to spare before the final pageant begins, Ms. Cheryl, dressed to kill in a leopard wrap dress and strappy leather stilettos, stops by Lauren's table to enlist help in controlling the flow of traffic for the entrance of queens. More than a thousand guests fill the tables lining either side of the grand aisle, but so many people have come to this year's crowning that additional rows of chairs have been added all the way to the back wall of the room. The queens will need some help as they navigate their way through this throng.

Ms. Cheryl doesn't know her well, but Lauren is an established presence on the festival circuit by this point, so she's a sure bet to understand what needs to happen. "See, I'm good for something," she tosses over her shoulder as she rises to take up station in the aisle. It's the first hint she's given all night that she wishes she could be out there, one of the girls, taking her final walk. It isn't Lauren's nature to be passive, so having a role of some kind is just her cup of tea. And now she gets to show off her sparkly black cocktail dress after all.

Lauren joins a half dozen other women lining the aisle for two purposes: to keep camera-happy Mamarazzi out of the traffic while the formal entry procession takes place, and to keep queens moving rapidly up the aisle, instead of stopping every few feet to pose. When a queen elongates her walk, the whole thing bottlenecks, which steals time in the spotlight from the girl behind her. That matters because, for seventy-one girls, this entrance will be their last of the night. As soon as they get assembled at the front, the Top 15 will be announced.

Chelsea enters, looking beautiful and singular in the more conservative of the two gowns she had considered. A criss-cross halter, half gem-studded and half ruched, tops a skirt flowing in teal and cream, with a gossamer train that floats away when she takes a step. It is a gorgeous dress that cost over a thousand dollars, money she didn't have after she quit her job at Buckle. Her dad bought the dress for her as a vote of confidence when she didn't give up her crown. Lauren works at a boutique and thinks if you're going to bother to spend money on a gown, it ought to be really fresh and really you. She gives this dress a thumbs-up.

Brandy wears the same gown she wore at her coronation, a green silk number that hangs perfectly and so suits her coloring that it seems as if had been designed just for her. It cost eight hundred dollars, a full month's pay. The first time she'd ever seen it, she'd handed over a two-week paycheck to hold it, then worked two more weeks, and came back after that payday with the rest of the money to bring the gown home. Lucky for her, there's only one other green dress in the pageant, so she makes a strong visual impression.

Kristen has perhaps the least chance of standing out. Maybe twenty of the girls here today are in blue, as she is, and a good sixty of them have brown hair (the Cajun gene pool not being awash in blondes). What does set her apart is how natural she seems. While many of the girls are now sporting hairstyles that make them look older or more sophisticated than they do when you meet them in a barn or on a Ferris wheel, Kristen's attitude toward pageant hair is, *No way, José.* She has pulled her hair back into a sleeker version of a ponytail, something Julia Roberts might wear, and that's it. And it isn't just about her look. While some of her competitors glide along as if on unseen tracks, she just bounds down the center aisle like a kid on a playground.

Lauren thinks this is the wrong setting for Kristen. "She is perfect for Cattle—they just need a real girl who's good with people. But these judges, not so much. They're going for polish." Lauren is not being mean, just reporting the facts, and, in truth, Kristen and her mom have both said the same thing. It's been clear since the moment they arrived that Queen of Queens is more like a traditional pageant, and Kristen just isn't a pageant girl.

The first finalist to be revealed is Yam, and the room fills with cheers. The waves of noise rise as she is joined onstage by Duck, another crowd favorite at evening gown prelims this morning. They are followed by Church Buggy, a girl who talked her neighbor into running for Beau Fair Queen last fall; both girls are here tonight. Though Church Buggy is more well-known to her fellow queens, seventeen-year-old Beau Fair made a big impression during this morning's evening gown prelims when she gracefully waited out a long pause after the emcee seemingly forgot her. Now Beau Fair joins her friend onstage, the pair having defied all odds to both place in the Top 15.

The emcee continues summoning finalists, titles ringing out: Forestry, whose bio says she likes four-wheeling and texting (hopefully not at the same time), and then River Parishes, about whom one audience member whispers, "She has a *perfect* Queen of Queens gown"—though the girl's current hairdo is slightly wider than the dress itself. Cal-Cam

Fair, whom Lauren had picked as a sure bet, is followed by Christmas on the Bayou, a teenager whose decision to miss softball practice today is now vindicated. When Allen Parish Fair is called, a chorus of her supporters yell, "Go, Rosie!" in unison, their ardor matched by the fans of Tournoi, a horse-riding queen and Student of the Year for her parish. Amite Oyster joins them, her offstage interview apparently having been more impressive than her bio, which lists "holding hands with my boyfriend" as an activity.

For the second year in a row, a Swamp Pop Queen makes the cut, but as the list goes on, newcomers crack the top tier as well. No Delcambre Shrimp representative has ever made Top 15 until now, nor has anyone from Courir de Mardi Gras, and this year's queen, still a high-school student, beams as she goes forward.

When the emcee says Cotton, and Brandy realizes that she has made it back into the Top 15 after all, she can breathe a little easier than she has all weekend. She lets go of the pressure that has been rising all afternoon, the fear that all the morning's chatter will have jinxed her. When she takes her place onstage, she is the picture of happy relief.

The Top 15 now stand onstage side by side as camera-wielding Mamarazzi jockey for the best sightlines and sixty-nine girls take their seats for the rest of the pageant—not seventy-one, for at least two newly relieved contestants won't be staying. Washington Catfish, resplendent in a snug red satin dress, hears and then feels something give way—and just like that, her beautiful gown splits open down the back, requiring her to exit *very* carefully, away from the crowd. And she isn't the only departure.

Kristen disappears through the ballroom doors in a flash of blue. One moment, her mom can see Kristen in the crowd of queens, and the next moment, she's gone. Lisa Hoover heads for the doors in time to see Ms. Denise heading out also. What on earth is going on? Kristen's brother, Matthew, and dad, Steven (who has gotten out of bed to come see her compete), follow Lisa and Ms. Denise into the hall and are soon joined by Chance, who is now an ex-ex. When Kristen, burning with fever, finishes throwing up in the bathroom, her concerned loved ones move like a tribe of nomads, their caravan heading for the emergency room.

While convention business takes over for a time, the Top 15 are sequestered in a side room, awaiting the call to return to the stage for the big question. They are nervous, some of them literally shaking, and several girls try to soothe their rattled peers. Beau Fair reminds everyone that this question is only a small part of their score, and Swamp Pop leads a prayer of thanks combined with a plea for calmed nerves. And then they're on.

Back in front of the crowd, they receive a prototypical pageant question: "Do you think celebrities should have any influence on today's young people?" Each queen is supposed to do two things: answer confidently and then model for the judges; some do better at one half of this equation than the other. Yam models flawlessly, but Lauren worries that her answer isn't quite on. Duck forgets to model entirely and then just ends up waving sheepishly at the judges.

As each girl takes her turn, a spotlight casts her shadow onto the back wall, yielding a billboard-sized silhouette. When it's Brandy's turn, the hall is pin quiet for her answer. "I'd like to think that celebrities don't have much influence but they do, in ways like the idea of the perfect body. Young ladies look up to them." Her voice doesn't betray her cold, and she doesn't hesitate at all. "We need better people to look up to, better *women*." There are lusty cheers when she finishes, but Lauren is nervous for her friend. It's a fine answer delivered well, but she worries that Brandy has missed a nuance of the question: The judges didn't ask *if* celebrities have influence, but whether they *should* have.

Even at this stage, with only fifteen girls left, the answers begin to run together in a stream. What stands out are rare moments of specificity—the only queen to provide a concrete illustration is Tournoi, who uses Michael Phelps as an example—as well as moments of unintended drama. Christmas on the Bayou begins by saying that anyone who is a role model "should prepare yourself and be yourself." She pauses. "In an orderly manner . . ." She takes a beat. And then another.

Across the aisle from my table, I hear her mother softly moan, "Oh, my poor baby . . ." Her daughter never quite finishes, but sympathetic applause follows the girl back to her spot in line.

Miles away, Kristen is surrounded by her coterie as the doctor diagnoses a bacterial infection that is going to require an immediate shot of antibiotics. In the butt. Missing your own pageant is one thing; missing it so that you can drop trou in front of your boyfriend and parents is something else entirely. She laughs nervously, considering that she is wearing a g-string, the standard underwear of choice for beneath an evening gown. "Uh, Doc, you know I'm in a thong, right?" He assures her that he's seen everything by this point, and gets the needle ready.

In the ballroom, three girls stand out as the questions wrap up. Shrimp is the first to link celebrities in general directly to the experience of festival queens. "They need to watch what they do, as a lot of young ladies look up to them just like us—young girls do look up to us." Beau Fair gets off to a slow start but earns cheers when she questions aloud why the media can't focus more on the *intelligence* of role models. Swamp Pop takes the opposite tack of every other contestant and argues that celebrities *should* have influence—what better way to use their fame? She is the picture of calm, all but for her fingertips, which play the air like a keyboard.

As the girls model for the judges one last time, the sound track takes them back decades, when the same music played for their mothers or even grandmothers. The nostalgic strains of "Moon River" and "Three Coins in the Fountain" add a sheen of melancholy just before the big finish. Lauren, understandably, has mixed emotions and smiles a rueful smile. "Honestly, sometimes I regret saying I wouldn't compete." But she shakes her head and straightens up. "Still, it was the right thing to do and I know that."

Months ago, Chelsea, Lauren, Kristen, and Brandy all set

out on their own paths leading here to this ballroom; as different from one another in affect and temperament as they are, a possible Queen of Queens existed within each. But here sits Lauren on the sidelines, a natural competitor who has agreed to be a spectator. Chelsea is now officially out of contention, too, though perhaps this was true even before she arrived. And poor Kristen isn't even in the building: She's texting from her gurney, wondering what's going on.

Only Brandy remains onstage, still living the drama, as the pageant finally resumes. After the effervescent Erath 4th of July Queen is named Miss Congeniality (a win that didn't require her to either make Top 15 or go knocking on doors), it is time for the Top 5. Unlike in some pageants, the final court is not separated out from the fifteen first. The fourth runner-up is called while all fifteen stand there, and then the rank moves upward one step at a time, so that when the ultimate title is about to be awarded, it doesn't come down to two girls holding hands—any one of the remaining girls can be called. Eleven girls may believe they are seconds away from being named Queen of Queens.

The fourth, third, and second runners-up are called: Lauren's early pick, the Calcasieu-Cameron Fair Queen; Delcambre Shrimp, the highest-placing queen ever from her festival; and River Parishes, the girl with the perfect queen's dress. Applause greets each one, but the drama really ramps up when the first runner-up is revealed to be Yam. The whistles and cheers of the crowd bounce off the stage as Yam accepts a bouquet the size of her torso. But her placement only heightens the mystery: As Yam was one of the odds-on favorites to win, the actual outcome seems all the less predictable.

Brandi Stout holds aloft the crown she is giving up as the emcee reads the name: Kacey Brister, Beau Fair! It's exactly the kind of outcome people love—unexpected but credible, the long shot that still makes perfect sense. No Beau Fair Queen has ever placed in the Top 5 here, much less won, so her victory comes with added distinction. Crowds of people who had never seen her before Thursday, many of whom haven't even heard of her fair, applaud as she does the equivalent of a deep-knee bend, so that she may be crowned by a girl seven inches shorter than she is. When the new Queen of Queens rises to full height, flushed and surprised and crying happily, her predecessor fans her with a paper plate to help cool her down so she doesn't faint in her moment of triumph. Across town, in the emergency room, Kristen gets the news by text.

At the front of the ballroom, queens are having pictures taken with the winner. While Chelsea poses with Kacey, the two so different in build that they look almost like different species, Brandy finds Lauren and me. She is disappointed, of course, after the roller coaster of the day's expectations—with all the praise she'd received, she couldn't entirely resist picturing the year ahead as Queen of Queens. But she is also proud of herself for having achieved the goal she set almost a year ago: getting back in shape, winning a title that meant something to her, and reclaiming her spot in the Top 15. Sure, she's sick and she's exhausted, but she earned the red pin even so. It will be a little heartbreaking when she learns later that she placed *sixth,* so close to breaking the Top 5, but tonight she is happy nonetheless. And both she and Lauren are honestly thrilled for Yam, whom they set off to find amid the throngs.

Ms. Cheryl and Miles are talking to Chelsea's parents, who are patiently waiting for their daughter to be done so they can say good-bye and start their hour-long drive back to Rayne. Ms. Cheryl wears a fat gold medallion, a kind of bling that isn't really her style, and Miles proudly holds up the plaque that accompanies the jewelry: Earlier this evening, LAFF named Ms. Cheryl Professional of the Year. But her win leaves her wistful. "I really thought Frog would win Best Festival this time. Don't get me wrong—I'm not giving this back. But it's not the same if just *I* win."

"Next year," Miles says.

And she laughs. "Damn straight!"

Chelsea joins us, marveling at the height of the new queen. "Did you see that? I don't reach past her shoulder! I couldn't put my head on it if I wanted to."

As her parents slowly make their escape through the still-swarming crowd, I tell Chelsea that she looks simply, purely, happy.

"You know, I am," she says. "After everything, I didn't really want to place because I knew it would bring more attention to me and my drama. I just wanted to walk in there looking confident and let my daddy see me wearing the pretty dress he bought me."

"So," I offer, "no need to go home and Google an inspirational saying?"

"No, sir, I'm going out to dinner instead!"

Chelsea and I are heading into the hallway when she tugs at my arm, as if just then remembering something really important, something that brings even more light into her face. It's a joy, a wonder, a fact no one can change.

"I'm *still* Frog Queen!"

Acknowledgments

This book would not have been possible without the four wonderful queens who let me observe their lives and tell their stories. A little bit Supremes and a little bit Charlie's Angels, Chelsea Richard, Lauren Naquin, Kristen Hoover, and Brandy Matulich became not only worthy subjects to write about, but dear friends.

I'd never have met any of them if I hadn't first talked to the Diva of Rayne, Cheryl McCarty. Once I met Cheryl, I knew I'd be coming back to her town a lot. I'm grateful to many of her fellow citizens, including Vicki and Errol Richard, Angie Broussard, Miles Boudreaux, Pesh Patel, Benoit Morel, Rusti Alleman, Robert Credeur, Nonc Randall, Kelsey and Paulette Primeaux, Monica and Byron Foote, and Maddie Guidry for welcoming me.

Across southern Louisiana, family members and directors of queens became important parts of my experience. All the Hoovers (including Grandma Helen, MeMaw, and PaPaw) and Dawn Childs made me feel like family. Thank you, directors

Denise Mire, Kelli Bueller, Brandi Zeringue, Paula Cappiello, Vicki Little, Amanda Thille, and Cindy Fontenot for bringing me into the world of your festivals. For contributions big and small in my Louisiana visits, thank you, Sondra Myrick, Jennifer Robicheaux, Hope Mestayer, Christana Goff, Brooke Henry, Charmaine Landry, Renee Berger, Lindsey Cooper, Ryan King, Joe Broussard, Curtis Hue, Barbara Horaist, Dayna Willis, Nicky Long, Millie Harris, Liz Landry, Susan Dore, Byron Blanchard, Guthrie Perry, Sallye LeBleu, Janice Guillroy, Phyllis Frazier, Geralynn Thomassee, Mae Mayeaux, the Menard family, Summer Parker, and Edward Leger. At the Wild Turkey Festival in Vinton, Ohio, I was given insight by Emily Ferguson, Brittany Marlowe, Joanna Schall, Chris Cramm, and Brandi Betts, as well as the Politician and the Preacher. At the Rhododendron Festival in Port Townsend, Washington, I was grateful for the chance to get to know Stacy Richards, Shawna-Kay Smith, Chelsea Benner, and Dana Perkins.

So many current and former festival queens and contestants shared stories or photos, filled out questionnaires, and offered help; I'm sorry I could not have included more of their lives in detail in this book. I can, at the very least, say thank you to Amanda Sullivan, Stevie Campbell, Meghin Frazier, Misty Picard, Blaine Nielsen, Lail DeLaunay, Angelle Thomassee, Gabrielle Theriot, Allyson Boudreaux, Kelli Sepulvado, Erin Husbands, Robin Sons, Brittany Soileau, Danielle Champagne, Kristen Abshire, Yuwa Vosper, Heather Hickey, Kaitlyn Yates, Heather Lynn Phillips, Megan Waguespack, Ashlei Tizeno, Danielle Herrell, Brandi Stout, Kacey Brister, Jeni Abrams,

Devin Babineaux, Nonnie Berard, Chelsea Troxler, Winter Duhon, Aimee Latour, Mariah Gewin, Leigh Phillips, and Heather Gonzalez.

I found the following publications useful in my research: Rayne *Advertiser,* Lafayette *Advertiser, Rayne Today,* Julie Avery's *Agricultural Fairs in America,* the *Shreveport Times,* the *El Granada Observer,* and the *Half Moon Bay Memories* Web site.

The research, the trips, the stories—none of this would have reached readers without the efforts of three people: Paul Cirone, my dazzling and delightful agent; Rachel Klayman, the force of energy who determined where this book would have its home; and Mary Choteborsky, whose deft edits and clear vision made every chapter shine more brightly.

I need to recognize indulgences for which I'm grateful. Because I like to write my first drafts in a public setting, I lingered for hours at Diesel Café, Bloc 11 Café, Crema Café, Porter Square Books, and the Arlington Center Starbucks. Also, for letting me go on and on about this topic while I worked, I thank my friends. (Mikey, Kristin, Abby, Ashley, Lauren, and Mike were especially long-suffering in this regard.)

I would never have finished this book without the love and support of my husband, Jason. He held down the fort at home, weekend after weekend, while I flew two thousand miles away to a corner of the world he has never even seen. He endured all my absences for the same reason I started the book in the first place: for the love of our little princess, Lily. In more ways than I can count, this book is for her.

ABOUT THE AUTHOR

DAVID VALDES GREENWOOD is a lecturer at Tufts University and a contributor to the *Boston Globe Magazine*. He is the author of two memoirs, *Homo Domesticus* and *A Little Fruitcake*.